The Triumph of
Value Investing

The Triumph of Value Investing

Smart-Money Tactics for the Postrecession Era

Janet Lowe

PORTFOLIO/PENGUIN

PORTFOLIO / PENGUIN
Published by the Penguin Group
Penguin Group (USA) Inc., 375 Hudson Street,
New York, New York 10014, U.S.A.
Penguin Group (Canada), 90 Eglinton Avenue East, Suite 700,
Toronto, Ontario, Canada M4P 2Y3
(a division of Pearson Penguin Canada Inc.)
Penguin Books Ltd, 80 Strand, London WC2R 0RL, England
Penguin Ireland, 25 St. Stephen's Green, Dublin 2, Ireland
(a division of Penguin Books Ltd)
Penguin Books Australia Ltd, 250 Camberwell Road, Camberwell,
Victoria 3124, Australia
(a division of Pearson Australia Group Pty Ltd)
Penguin Books India Pvt Ltd, 11 Community Centre, Panchsheel Park,
New Delhi – 110 017, India
Penguin Group (NZ), 67 Apollo Drive, Rosedale, North Shore 0632,
New Zealand (a division of Pearson New Zealand Ltd)
Penguin Books (South Africa) (Pty) Ltd, 24 Sturdee Avenue,
Rosebank, Johannesburg 2196, South Africa

Penguin Books Ltd, Registered Offices:
80 Strand, London WC2R 0RL, England

First published in 2010 by Portfolio / Penguin,
a member of Penguin Group (USA) Inc.

10   9   8   7   6   5   4   3   2   1

Publisher's Note
This publication is designed to provide accurate and authoritative information in regard to the subject matter covered. It is sold with the understanding that the publisher is not engaged in rendering legal, accounting or other professional services. If you require legal advice or other expert assistance, you should seek the services of a competent professional.

Library of Congress Cataloging-in-Publication Data

Lowe, Janet.
   The triumph of value investing : smart-money tactics for the post-recession era / Janet Lowe.
      p. cm.
   Includes bibliographical references and index.
   ISBN 978-1-59184-374-0
   1. Value investing.   2. Investment analysis.   3. Stocks.   I. Title.
   HG4521.L828 2010
   332.6—dc22   2010022346

Printed in the United States of America
Set in Minion
Designed by Alissa Amell

Dedicated to Alan and my entire family, for their patience and loyalty.

Contents

The Triumph of
Value Investing

Introduction

The past decade has been a trying but an instructive one for investors: first the dot-com bubble burst between 2000 and 2002, then all the world's stock markets crashed in 2007–8. Almost all investors, regardless of their philosophies, were bloodied. Even many value investors, the most conservative and stable of the bunch, felt the force of the hurricane.

Until they realized how quickly their holdings were rebounding, value investors may have questioned whether their principles still applied.

During the bull markets of the early twenty-first century, Warren Buffett's Berkshire Hathaway Inc., a holding company operated on value principles, was not the most stellar performer on the stock market and was the darling only of Berkshire's loyal shareholders. More than thirty thousand enthusiastic followers show up at Berkshire's annual meeting each year to cheer Buffett on. They ended up on the victorious team. In 2009 Buffett's company turned in one of the best performances in its amazing forty-five-year history. The company's net worth increased by $21.8 billion and the per-share book value of its stock rose by 19.8 percent.

Another value investor, Seth Klarman, has outperformed the market consistently over a long period, without using leverage or short selling. During the past twenty-five years, his company The Baupost Group has generated an annual compound return of 20 percent and is ranked forty-ninth in *Alpha's* hedge fund rankings. In the pages ahead you will read about these and many more value investors who have either preserved principal or triumphed in very difficult market conditions.

It is always healthy to check up on the validity of your own thinking. Considering the market breakdowns of the past decade, the discouragement many individual investors have suffered, and new federal laws, this is an excellent time to restudy Benjamin Graham's concepts of value investing and learn how to apply them to a whole range of new challenges.

It is time to look at how the principles work and how they can be changed or improved for a world that is technology oriented, virtually borderless, and moving at the speed of electrons.

I first wrote about Professor Graham as a newspaper investment columnist in the 1980s. My original book on the subject, *Benjamin Graham on Value Investing* (Dearborn), was published in 1994 and my second, *Value Investing Made Easy* (McGraw-Hill), came out in 1996. This began a deepening interest in value ideals and those who practice this form of investing. While value investing has been called a "formula" by some, I didn't see it that way. Graham himself was curious, experimental, and always looking for new and better ways to apply basic principles.

The Triumph of Value Investing: Smart-Money Tactics for the Postrecession Era returns to that familiar ground. The book will walk investors through the steps necessary to determine intrinsic value, identify a margin of safety, and apply the other guidelines that define value investing. It celebrates the sound principles and deep truths underlying Graham's concepts.

Whether a reader is familiar with value investing or is just discovering what superinvestor Warren Buffett calls the village of "Graham and Doddsville," there will be plenty of fresh information in *The Triumph of Value Investing*. The book covers the latest concepts and players in the market. It takes into consideration ideas, industry developments, experiences, and company stories that have occurred in the past decade or so. It addresses the issue of investing in high technology, biotech, and foreign companies, and explains the use of products such as index funds and exchange traded funds (ETFs). Additionally, the book guides the investor to Internet resources to gather information for analysis, support decisions, make purchases, and manage portfolios. Most of all, the book recognizes that financial advisers of various types and government regulators may never be able to adequately protect our money. While advisers and governments are important and should be accountable, we also must learn to take care of ourselves as much as we can. The best defense is knowledge.

This book is written for individual investors, whether those investors want to manage their own money or simply to better understand how their money is being handled.

Please refer to the glossary at the back of the book for more detail if there are terms you don't understand. Even when a subject is discussed within a chapter, reading the definition of the terms involved may lead to a deeper understanding. The reading list and compendium of useful Internet sites will lead to information that will deepen your understanding of the investment world and help you to develop the type of intuition that Warren Buffett and others have found indispensable.

The Triumph of Value Investing includes interviews with current, leading value investors such as Warren Buffett, William O'Neil, David Iben, Charles Brandes, Alan Bradford, and others. I would like to thank these people for the time they spent talking to me and for their passion for investing. Also, thanks to my literary representative, Alice Martell, my editor, Courtney Young, and Matthew Boezi and Alissa Amell at Portfolio Penguin who made this book possible.

Most of all please enjoy the book. Investing, after all, is one of the most fascinating exercises there is and should be fun.

Janet Lowe
Santa Fe, New Mexico, 2010

Chapter 1

Value Investing in Troubled Times

I could not, at any age, be content to take my place by the fireside, and simply look on. Life was meant to be lived. Curiosity must be kept alive.

ELEANOR ROOSEVELT

People everywhere entered the twenty-first century feeling more optimistic, wiser, richer, and more in control than at any other time in recent history. This was especially true for Americans. For seventy years the U.S. economy had grown at a steady pace, generating ever-higher incomes, standards of living, and wealth levels. Despite the way we started, however, it has been a rocky century for investors so far. The signs of turmoil came quickly in the new millennium.

Powered by the indiscriminate creation of Internet companies and excessive exuberance in high technology in general, the dot-com bubble popped with near-devastating effects in 2000 and 2001. So-called prefix investing was rampant as newly formed companies were seeing their stock prices shoot up by simply adding an "e-" prefix to their name or a ".com" at the end.

Some big dreams came crashing down after March 10, 2000, when the technology-heavy NASDAQ Composite Index peaked at 5,048.62, more than double its value just a year earlier. The next Monday, multibillion dollars' worth of sell orders for major bellwether high-tech stocks such as Cisco, IBM, and Dell hit the exchange. This initiated a chain reaction as investors, funds, and institutions liquidated positions. Within six days the NASDAQ lost nearly 9 percent, falling to 4,580 by March 15. By October 2002 the dot-com correction wiped out $5 trillion in market value for technology stocks, helping to trigger a mild economic recession.

A Second Tsunami Hits Wall Street

Most investors did not seem to hear the warning shot; within a very few years the Web 2.0 movement sparked a fresh round of venture capital and initial public offering (IPO) investing and speculation.

Investors suffered blows from other directions as well. In the early 2000s, shareholders in major public corporations such as Enron, Tyco, Adelphia, and WorldCom lost billions of dollars due to deceptive and criminally inaccurate financial statements. In response to the massive corporate and accounting fraud, Congress passed the Sarbanes–Oxley Act of 2002 (SOX), but the new law did not fully prevent original and innovative forms of financial deception. There have been many famous bank robbers; soon the world would learn all about robber banks.

The Third Killer Wave

But again, we all felt remarkably smart and secure when the stock market doubled in just a decade, from 7,022 in February 1997 to 14,164 in October 2007. But that was the top and just seventeen months later, by March 2009, all that new wealth had gone up in smoke. The Dow Jones Industrial Average (DJIA) had plummeted 53 percent to 6,547. Some global markets fared better than others, but overall world stock market capitalization dove more than 32 percent in about eighteen months. By January 2010 the market still hadn't recovered fully, although at around 10,000 the DJIA was nearly halfway back to its former peak. What a comeuppance this had been.

Some pundits call the era the econolypse, while others dub it the crecession—a combination of credit crisis and recession. Although the U.S. economy officially fell into recession in December 2007, it is tough to pin the downward plunge to a single year. Cracks in mortgage markets and corporate credit problems began early in 2007 and continued with sluggish national output and high unemployment through 2010.

Drawing parallels between our current situation and the Great Depression of the 1920s and 1930s is irresistible. However, present conditions haven't been as dire as they were back then. Unemployment during that period reached 25 percent, while in 2009 it peaked at around 10 percent. In the Great Depression the stock market nose-dived by 86 percent before hitting bottom in 1932. The DJIA did not return to pre-1929 levels until November 1954.

While the stock market behavior in 2007–8 can more accurately be compared with the market decline of 1973–74, it appears that the U.S. economic situation may have been as precarious as it was prior to the Great Depression and the nationwide sense of panic was nearly as severe.

"It's the only out and out panic I've seen," said William O'Neil, founder of *Investor's Business Daily*, who has been in the business for five decades. "People were saying, was my money safe in Bank of America."

The first decade of the new millennium ended sadly for many people, and yet as in all financial crises, some people profited, others saw opportunities for future profit, and we all learned important lessons. It is thus a perfect time to revisit the principles of value investing, and see how they work for us and how they should be fine-tuned or amended in what seems like a financial environment, despite new laws, that will continue to be challenging for some time to come.

No matter how we were affected, no matter whom we blame, no matter what changes we demand in the system, we each have the responsibility to take care of our own resources, move along, improve our situations, and do what each of us can to prevent a repeat of history.

In May 2009 *Wall Street Journal* columnist Jason Zweig wrote, "At this moment, consulting Mr. Graham's wisdom is especially fitting."[1] Zweig went on to declare that in present market conditions, Graham would no doubt go about his own analysis calmly, ignoring the ranting and raving so often heard, especially among financial television drama kings and queens.

Taking Responsibility

William O'Neil stresses the importance of taking responsibility for our own money. Most individuals work hard, save, and then hope they can turn their entire life savings over to someone else to manage. Getting help is okay and for many people it makes sense to turn to some kind of financial expert, but even then, in order to protect themselves, investors need to know the basics of economics, how business operates, and something about the securities markets and evaluating individual securities. "Education is needed. Anyone can learn it if they are willing to do the work. You learn an awful lot by getting in there and studying it," insists O'Neil.

On its Web site, the Securities and Exchange Commission warns: "The world of investing is fascinating and complex, and it can be very fruitful. But unlike the banking world, where the federal government guarantees deposits, stocks, bonds and other securities can lose value. There are no guarantees. That's why investing is not a spectator sport.

By far the best way for investors to protect the money they put into the securities markets is to do research and ask questions."

Rebuilding the Financial Fortress

The earlier review of history won't comfort people who've lost so much of their personal wealth and their hopes and dreams for the future, including a secure retirement. Yet given the historic performance of the stock markets and the threat of high inflation presented by global economy recovery efforts, there is nothing to do but get back in the savings and investing game and learn from the first big crash of the new millennium. That's what this book is about, a postmortem, or as the military calls it, a hot wash. This is a "lessons learned" exercise about what happened, and then a game plan for moving along to recovery and protecting our capital in the future.

This is a book for those like Eleanor Roosevelt, who can't sit by on the sidelines. This is for people who believe in capitalism and want to actively participate in a way that brings the best possible outcome for all players.

We can rebuild what was lost and fortify what we have by turning to the basic value principles that underlie all financial investments as taught by the brilliant investor and legendary Columbia University professor Benjamin Graham. We can maneuver sanely through any type and duration of turmoil, and as Graham taught, with the proper mind-set, we can even benefit from such disruptions.

As Daniel Myers wrote in *Forbes* in February 2009, "Graham's basic ideas are timeless and essential for long-term success. He bought into the notion of buying stocks based on the underlying value of a business and turned it into a science at a time when almost all investors viewed stocks as speculative."[2]

It may be no accident that Graham, whose academic background and lifelong interest was in languages, mathematics, and not least, philosophy, should choose the word "value" to describe his investment approach. Philosophers tell us that the concept of value and questions regarding value run deep and apply to every aspect of life. What gives anything genuine value? What is truly worth yearning for, working for, and keeping in our lives? The questions apply to money as much as they do to family, friends, culture, or anything else. The financial world operates within the real world and does not escape the question of value.

Lasting Influence

Graham was the best-known and most respected investor of his time. The father of value investing, Graham remains a guiding light in the investment world nearly fifty years after his death. Two of his books, *Security Analysis* and *The Intelligent Investor*, are considered classics, although their style and the examples in them come from a time gone by.

Nevertheless, Graham experienced many of the same market dramas that we currently face. He began his career on Wall Street prior to the crash of 1929, before the stock market had much regulation and before the enactment of accounting procedures and disclosure laws that exist today. It was an era of speculation, manipulation, and insider trading.

Learn from the Masters

Among those who studied under Graham and still stick to his principles are the greatly admired Warren Buffett, Walter Schloss, and Irving Kahn. Graham's faithful disciples include John Bogle, David Dreman,

Seth Klarman, Peter Lynch, Mario Gabelli, John Neff, Charles Brandes, Bill Miller, Michael O'Neill, Michael F. Price, and Michael Whitman, distinguished investors all. The notable but deceased Christopher Browne, John Templeton, William Ruane, and Max Heine also are among them. The band of followers is much larger, of course, and in the past quarter century the family of value investors has spread all over the world. At one time Buffett held a special reception at the Berkshire Hathaway annual meeting for investors from other countries. The number of foreign investors grew so large that in 2010 he had to discontinue the event.

There are numerous critics of value investing. Some feel that the best way to maximize stock market returns is to emphasize growth, despite the added risk. Other market gurus say the road to riches is to understand and profit from economic cycles. Proponents of modern portfolio theory claim that it is impossible for any individual investor to outsmart the stock market. Others get a greater kick from the excitement of market timing and day trading.

Nevertheless, a legion of academic studies appearing in publications such as *The Journal of Finance* and *The Financial Analyst's Journal* and by organizations like the Brandes Institute keep driving home the message that value stocks outperform the market over nearly all multiyear periods. Value investing principles continue to hold up; in fact they provide balance, stability, and an investor's best hope for building lasting, reliable wealth regardless of market conditions.

While it is true that Warren Buffett's value-based holding company Berkshire Hathaway declined in share price in some years, it has maintained its worth much better than the S&P 500. The S&P has been in negative territory two of the past five years, while Berkshire's share price has declined only one year in the past five. While Berkshire's per-share book value varies, over the past forty-five years Buffett has outgrown the S&P book value by an annual average of

11.4 percent. By early 2010 Berkshire shares were trading at more than $125,000, up from the fifty-two-week low of $79,800. At their peak the shares traded for more than $140,000 each.

Other value investors also have demonstrated the advantages of the methodology. The American Association of Individual Investors prepares model portfolios each year using screens for different investment philosophies. In the first half of 2009 many of the portfolio share prices showed negative or lagging growth. Yet the value investing portfolio provided a yield of 40.9 percent, and the Schloss portfolio, also value based, gave a return of 30.8 percent. This compares with a 19 percent return for the growth portfolio and 18.5 percent for index-based portfolios. However, when value principles were applied with special attention to growth indicators, as will be described in chapter 9, the half-year return was 67.1 percent.

Simply put, the value-investing approach focuses on buying securities whose shares seem to be underpriced for some reason. Value investing involves fundamental analysis, along with the concept of looking for a margin of safety.

Graham's Key Concepts

The stock market of the 1920s and 1930s seemed illogical and impossible to predict, but Graham realized that beneath the chaos, there was order. He pointed out that each security represented a real company and that company had a value, just as a house or a horse or a hat would have an appropriate value. He wanted to know the right price if you set out to buy the entire company, and then he divided that price by the number of shares outstanding to determine the correct share price. That may sound like common sense, but nobody invested that way in Graham's time, and interestingly, only a small group of people invest that way today.

Graham warned fifty years ago that investors should never try to anticipate stock market movements—that's a loser's game. However, investors can protect themselves against losses and take advantage of depressed stock prices to add valuable stocks to their portfolios.

The Ben Graham Story: Learning from Adversity

Benjamin Graham grew up in a time of cataclysmic technological and social change and market volatility. The telephone, automobile, and electricity as a generally used source of power were invented earlier but were just coming into common usage. Airplane travel was becoming a reality. But the stock market crash of 1929 shocked him and rocked his life as much as it did any other occurrence.

Graham was born in London in 1894, and when he was an infant his family immigrated to New York. Soon after arriving his father died, leaving his mother to raise three sons. The family was poor, but thanks to his diligence and intelligence, Graham won a scholarship to Columbia University. There he excelled in languages, mathematics, and philosophy. He expected to become a professor, but to Graham's surprise, when he graduated his dean arranged for him to join an investment firm. He knew nothing about Wall Street when he showed up for work in 1914.

Almost immediately Europe went to war and markets in Europe and the United States went dark. The New York Stock Exchange was closed for more than four months, but trading did not stop. A sort of flea market for stocks, or a "gutter market," moved outside the exchange, and both action and prices were literally in the gutter. When the NYSE finally reopened, trading went wild. America entered the war on March 17, 1917, and by November of that year, the market had plunged 31 percent. "It looked like the end of the world had happened," Graham explained in a 1975 *Forbes* interview, "but after a year and a half we were in a raging bull market."[3]

Graham quickly caught on to the ways of Wall Street and came up with innovative methods of making money for clients. By the 1920s he was managing money on his own, successful and full of self-confidence.

The salad days again ended abruptly come the autumn of 1929. Graham's daughter recalled that the family was forced to move from a lavish Park Avenue apartment to more modest digs. Despite his brilliance, Graham's clients went down with everyone else. Ben and his partner Jerome Newman toiled for five years without salaries until their clients were again made whole.

During the desperate years, Graham began teaching investment classes uptown at Columbia University to help meet expenses. He asked another finance professor, David Dodd, to attend his seminars and to keep notes. In 1934 the notes were published in *Security Analysis,* the book that first laid out the principles of value investing. The book is now considered a classic, the beacon by which many investors have sustained profits for the duration of their careers.

When Graham first began writing and teaching, he gave no particular name to his concepts. His intention was simple: to present a logical, reality-based approach to stocks and the companies they represented.

Once the Graham Newman Corporation portfolio had recovered from the losses of the 1929 crash, Graham never again lost money for his clients. Over a thirty-year period that included the crash, the Great Depression, and two world wars, Graham's clients earned an average annual return of around 17 percent. That did not include returns from his most famous investment discovery, the Government Employees Insurance Co. (GEICO). More about GEICO in later chapters.

Graham retired in 1956 and referred many of his clients to an eager and talented young friend and protégé, Warren Buffett. Graham's people became early investors in Berkshire Hathaway Inc., and many of their children and grandchildren still own the stock today. Graham died in 1976 at his second home at Aix in the South of France. He was eighty-two.

Graham encouraged investors to think for themselves, act independently, and keep asking questions. As a result of endless observation and research, Graham came up with three key concepts that hold true for investors of all times.

Buffett and others who study Graham's teachings have impressive analytical skills, but they still live and invest by these three baseline principles: the right attitude, margin of safety, and determining intrinsic value. We will explore these concepts in more detail in chapter 2.

To be fair, most individual investors are no longer sure how to calculate or even approximate the true worth, or intrinsic value, of the stocks they are considering buying. There is little doubt that recent economic troubles will continue to rock investors far into the future. This could be both a blessing and a burden. On the worrisome side:

- The federal government may continue to be co-owner of certain companies for quite some time.

- The capital gains tax rate may increase.

- There will be heavier government regulation in several industries.

- Inflation will rise.

On the positive side, shareholders may:

- have a stronger voice in setting executive pay

- become more focused on preserving capital

- manage their debt wisely

- discover new and better ways to oversee their finances

- be more aware of what constitutes fraud

The following trends are well under way, but investors may fully realize that we will emerge from the current mess as an even more global economy and that technology is firmly entrenched in our financial lives.

Yes, the Times They Are A'Changin

The changes that have taken place since Graham's time seem to have accelerated in the twenty-first century.

We're in a phase of rapid and wrenching transition, moving from national economies to a fully global economy, from a world that moved mostly in the physical realm to one that also lives and operates on electronic devices and within the invisible world of the Internet. The movement from heavy industry into intellectual property–based companies keeps investors guessing. While transportation of people and goods and delivery of services continue to be important, we need to think about the impact of technologies in these fields and their relevance when so much of what we need is bought, sold, or delivered electronically. The global revolution and the digital/communications/Internet revolution are closely intertwined and are creating a borderless world for individuals, governments, businesses, and particularly for investors. The turmoil we are experiencing is not new. The times are similar to a number of other technology-inspired revolutions of the past, including the advent of railroads in the 1840s, automobiles in the early 1900s, the invention of the radio in the 1920s, and transistor electronics in the 1950s.

So much is new and yet so much has remained the same, especially in the behavior related to investment markets. Groupthink dominates almost all aspects of financial markets. The madness of crowds is all around us. The instability of currencies is worrisome and gold remains emotionally and culturally charged.

There are many challenging questions. How do we preserve the power of capitalism yet curb its abuses? Where will we be able to earn money? What will be the next big idea? Where will our money be safe from loss of principal and the erosion of inflation?

Where We're Headed

The chapters ahead will address those and many other questions. In chapters 2 and 3 we will learn more about value investing in general, then in the following chapters we will discuss the basic value principles and explore the ways they work and how they can be adapted to the economic atmosphere as it exists today.

Graham calmly and rationally applied and refined his value principles in all economic climates. He applied the principles to all classes of securities, including preferred stocks, municipal bonds, corporate bonds, and all types of mutual funds. Each of these investment categories on its own deserves an entire book, but in this book we will only discuss them as they relate to value investing. Our primary focus here will be common stocks, the most available form of equity ownership in the corporate realm, although we often will refer, contrast, and compare with the other investment categories as well.

Chapter 2

Value Investing in the Twenty-first Century

Successful investing is all about common sense.

JOHN C. BOGLE, FOUNDER AND FORMER
CEO OF THE VANGUARD MUTUAL FUND GROUP[1]

There is no better example of the wisdom of following Benjamin Graham's teaching than his most famous disciple, Warren Buffett. In the several years leading up to the crash, many commentators were talking about how Buffett had lost his edge, how his Berkshire Hathaway wasn't performing with the muscle it once had shown. At the start of 2009 pundit Douglas Kass declared that Buffett's "salad days" were over.[2]

Yet, as pointed out in the last chapter, even though Berkshire Hathaway is so large it no longer is nimble, the holding company continues its remarkable performance. Once again, those anxious to make money fast had underestimated Buffett. Within months the same critics began to realize that Buffett had patiently collected a pile of cash awaiting a buyer's market. He granted a huge loan to Goldman Sachs and got a 10 percent annual return, plus an option to buy 43.5 million shares of Goldman at $115 per share. In less than a year those shares were selling for around $170. He helped out General Electric, Mars candy, and Dow Chemical, but at a price advantageous to his own shareholders. He added to positions in Wells Fargo, U.S. Bancorp, BNSF, and other holdings. Although Buffett continued to make moves that baffled some professional investors, 2009 turned out to be one of the best years in his six decades of working with money.

Value Investing Versus Technical Analysis

Value investing uses a form of fundamental analysis, which only has a passing relationship with the more distant and abstract technical analysis. Technical analysts do not attempt to measure a security's value in terms of the company's actual worth to owners, but instead use statistics related to market activity, charts, and other tools to identify trading patterns that can suggest future activity. Technical analysts believe that past performance is an indicator of future behavior. They work with cycles, patterns, momentum, and other data to look into the crystal ball of future share price activity.

"In a shopping mall," explains Investopedia, "a fundamental analyst would go to each store, study the product that was being sold, and then decide whether to buy it or not. By contrast, a technical analyst would sit on a bench in the mall and watch people go into the stores. Disregarding the intrinsic value of the products in the store, the technical analyst's decision would be based on the patterns of activity of people going into each store."[3]

In some ways the modern value investors combine technical analysis with the fundamental approach. Value investing blends qualitative and quantitative methodologies. To Graham's way of thinking quantitative factors, or the numbers, trumped qualitative features, or factors that are mainly situational. However, he also knew that qualitative elements can offer a significant margin of safety and in special circumstances can take center stage. When choosing between similar securities, the qualitative factors could provide the information that tips the scale toward one corporate share or away from another.

As explained in the previous chapter, in a very broad sense, value investors are trying to approach the investment markets with the right attitude, determine the intrinsic value of the securities they find there, and buy those securities at a price that allows a comfortable margin of safety.

The Right Attitude

Investing, according to value practitioners, is not a game of chance. It is a game of fact-based strategy. Value investors look to the businesses that are represented by the shares trading on the stock exchange. They then study those businesses as if they were going to buy the whole company.

Value investors are cognizant of market swings, but do not "play the market." They know that share price fluctuates continually, but pay attention to price movements only as an opportunity to buy low and sell high. We will delve into that subject more deeply in chapter 4.

Mario Gabelli developed this concept into a widely followed method that he calls private-market value. He describes private-market value as intrinsic value with an added control premium. Gabelli's company has $30 billion in client assets under management and has delivered a compound annual growth rate for investors of 19.3 percent.

Buffett often repeats similar advice: "Chapter 8 of *The Intelligent Investor*, that chapter's worth every other textbook put together. It's having the right attitude, not great skills, not knowing calculus, it's an attitude that's fundamentally sound. It doesn't require a master's degree, but settling into investments."

Value investing, Graham taught, is a hunt for securities selling below their intrinsic value, which are then held until there is some compelling reason to sell them.

"An investment operation," wrote Graham, "is one which, upon thorough analysis, promises safety of principal and an adequate return. Operations not meeting these requirements are speculation."

- Safety of Principal—Your investment is more likely to be safe if the enterprise is on a sound financial terrain and has a high-quality management team in place.

- Adequate Return—Since future return is based on earnings, an adequate return will depend on the company's present and future prospects. What is the company earning now and what is its earning potential? The total return—potential or actual—must compare favorably to that available from other relatively safe investments.

Intrinsic Value

Benjamin Graham was not the first to coin the term "intrinsic value." It was used in reference to corporate stock as early as 1848. Investment writer William Armstrong described it as the main determinant in establishing the market price of securities, although for Armstrong it was not the only factor.

Intrinsic value can be an elusive and ever-changing quantity. Different analysts use different measures of intrinsic value, all of which we will explore in future chapters. For example, net current asset value was a favorite tool of Ben Graham. The search for intrinsic value can take you down many paths and to many places. The balance sheet will give indications of safety, while the income statement gives clues to future growth.

Buffett once explained, "What counts is intrinsic value, a number that is impossible to pinpoint but essential to estimate." Buffett went on to add, "We define intrinsic value as the discounted value of the cash that can be taken out of a business during the remaining life."[4] In other words, he is basing his decision on the future earnings power of the company, adjusted for inflation.

A share can change its position in relation to intrinsic value for several reasons, including (sadly) a decline in asset value, or (happily) an increase in the price of the shares. Graham warned that investors cannot know when a stock will rise to or above intrinsic value, but only need to rest assured that it will, in time, do so. When a security you own is trading above its intrinsic value, or when competing investments offer a greater return, it is time to sell. Market factors do not dominate such decisions, but they cannot be ignored.

Mr. Dow and His Theory

Charles H. Dow was the pioneering founder and editor of *The Wall Street Journal*. He became famous for his study of stock market movements, and the Dow Theory, not to mention the company (Dow Jones) and many indices that bear his name.

Despite the findings of Dow's research, he and Graham were not that far apart in their beliefs. Dow often explained to his readers that shares rise and fall in reaction to investors' expectations of the future profitability of the underlying company.

In May 1900 Dow wrote: "It is always safe to assume that values determine prices in the long run. Values have nothing to do with current fluctuations. A worthless stock can go up five points just as easily as the best, but as a result of continued fluctuations the good stock will eventually work to its investment value, while the poor one will gradually go to its value as a gambling counter or perhaps with reference to its voting power for control."[5]

"Dow started his career as an investigative reporter, specializing in business and finance," explains Richard Russell, editor of the Dow Theory Letters. "In 1885 (and few people are aware of this), Dow became a member of the New York Stock Exchange, and this provided him with an intimate knowledge of how the market works. In 1889 Dow began publishing a little newspaper that he called *The Wall Street Journal*. Between 1899 and 1902 Dow wrote a series of editorials for his *Journal*, columns that many consider among the finest ever to come out of Wall Street. Written almost 100 years ago, these editorials are as pertinent and valuable today as they were the day they were written."[6]

The Dow Theory is a market timing method that relies on specific market configurations for buy and sell signals. According to the theory, these signals are confirmed when one average follows the behavior of another.

While the Dow Theory has called market movements in some stretches of time, it has not been reliable over the long haul. For the thirty-year period between 1938 and 1968, for example, Graham's research showed that Dow Theory investors would have fared much better simply buying and holding the DJIA. This was one of the ideas that led to the creation of index funds.

Dow became *The Wall Street Journal*'s primary stock market columnist in 1898. He died just four years later. Considering his short tenure in business journalism, Dow's influence on the investment world has been vast.

It seems apparent that most individual investors, even serious, dedicated students of investing, are no longer confident about calculating the true worth, or intrinsic value, of the stocks they are considering buying. It seems to them that so much has changed in the world of finance. Tax accounting rules are complicated. There are many new and complex securities to consider; the Internet puts an incredible amount of information before us at the click of a key, and allows trading at lightning speed. On top of that, there is a new global economy, as demonstrated by the creation of the European Community (now European Union) and the rise of Asia and what once were considered third-world nations.

Take a deep breath and settle down. Companies are still companies, and the principles that applied in the past and in Western cultures apply to companies everywhere. Political governance may change, law may change, taxes may be amended, but if you can find basic, accurate numbers, two and two still equal four.

Margin of Safety

"I do not know of many economists who accurately predicted the macroeconomic climate over the past year," wrote Ravi Nagarajan, "and there are virtually no stock market forecasters who predicted 50 percent declines in the major averages. I certainly did not anticipate the market carnage and I have no faith in my ability to know where the Dow or S&P will be at this time next year. Rather than attempting to forecast the economy or the direction of the overall market, it makes sense to identify individual securities that trade at levels that provide a solid margin of safety."[7] The margin of safety invariably is found within the company you are considering buying, or has been lost in the company you wish to sell.

The term "margin of safety" is frequently heard in discussions of value investing. It's a simple concept. If you buy a house, for example, at a price below its appraised value, or for less than other buyers are paying for the same size and type of home, you are taking less risk. If perchance you need to sell the house, the odds are better that you will be able to get a similar or even higher price than you paid. The same would be true for an automobile if purchased at a discount, and it also is true for stock purchases. Value investors look for bargains, or shares selling below their true value. The difference between the purchase price and the actual value of the item is the margin of safety.

There are various ways to identify this safety net. Graham sought a margin of safety in three primary areas:

- Evaluation of assets

- Analysis of earning power

- Diversification

These are not the only methods of building a margin of safety. Safety can also be found in a substantial stash of corporate working capital; in a strong, positive cash flow; and even in a company's consistently strong dividend history.

Ben Graham emphasized the need for safety measures because of his early experiences in the stock market. Seth Klarman explained to his shareholders that vigilance remains an essential element of safety. "You must always be prepared for the unexpected, including sudden, sharp downward swings in markets and the economy," observed Klarman. "Whatever adverse scenario you can contemplate, reality can be far worse."[8]

What Are the Chances?

There is little doubt that the economic woes of the early twenty-first century will continue to worry investors far into the future. Buffett notes that the nation has been through the financial equivalent of Pearl Harbor. As explained earlier, crises such as that can be both a blessing and a burden. Citizens may question the importance of capitalism and either overreact or underreact when seeking reforms. Again, while government participation in private business is common in other cultures, such as Chinese businesses and Airbus SAS in Europe, it makes Americans uncomfortable. Due to the government's need to increase tax revenue, the U.S. capital gains tax rate may increase somewhat and there may be heavier government regulation in the financial and other industries. On the positive side, shareholders could come away stronger and wiser; investors may become more focused on preserving capital; they should be more aware of what constitutes fraud; and certainly we all should understand the danger of debt.

Neutral but of enormous consequence, as we emerge from the current mess the economy will become even more global and we will be progressively more technological. These and many other factors must be measured in terms of how they affect investment analysis and results.

Investors will recover and even thrive after the madness of 2007–8. Near the end of 2009 Charles Brandes told me, "The extreme bargains, and they were extreme, of March 2009 are not there anymore. However, there are still, in equity markets worldwide, lots of good opportunities if you are patient, if you don't worry about market fluctuations, and if you think about the long-term earnings these companies will have."

Brandes also pointed out that investors were reacting to the pain of recent experiences and avoiding some key industries such as financial, telecommunications, and pharmaceutical stocks. These are key industries, he noted, and there were many opportunities for growth within them.

Mario Gabelli told his investors there were many value plays at the end of the first decade of the new century. For example, despite, or perhaps because of, President Obama's focus on developing alternative forms of energy, he saw opportunity in public utilities. As he traditionally has, Gabelli was investing in large companies with strong balance sheets and no debt, as well as small and microcap companies that had been "ignored and unloved."

Chapter 3

Virtues and Vices of
Graham's Philosophy

*To achieve satisfactory investment results is easier than most people
realize; to achieve superior results is harder than it looks.*

BENJAMIN GRAHAM[1]

S keptics of value investing come back to the same questions we've
asked in earlier chapters: How can principles first put forth in the
1930s, in the days when information moved by snail mail, telegraph,
or at the very best by telephone, be relevant today? There was no direct
trading on the stock market then, nor was there program trading.
Information on companies was filed away in dark repositories and was
difficult to ferret out. There were a tiny number of foreign companies in
the mix, and mathematicians and statisticians spent little time coming
up with new stock market theories. Today we live in a more transparent,
fast-moving, savvy global economy. Don't mutual funds, hedge funds,
and the big dogs have an unbeatable edge over everyone else? How can
individual investors hold their own under such circumstances?

The picture is not as hopeless as it might appear. Warren Buffett
explains that while it is true that people have more information available
to them, "new information and new technology isn't important, really."
He adds that even though a massive amount of data on companies and
their share performance is available, most people don't seem to use it.
And it always comes back to a basic concept: "If you own the right business," Buffett says, "you're basically going to make money in this world."

As Graham pointed out more than four decades ago, the small investor actually has certain advantages over anyone who is managing a large pool of money and likely to be involved in rapid trades or program trading.

"I am convinced that an individual investor with sound principles, and soundly advised, can do distinctly better over the long pull than a large institution," Graham claimed. "Where the trust company has to confine its operation to 300 concerns or less, the individual has up to 3000 issues for his investigations and choice. Most true bargains are not available in large blocks; by this very fact, the institutions are well nigh eliminated as competitors of the bargain hunter."[2]

Today small investors have an even larger investment universe, plus products such as index funds and exchange traded funds that can broaden the base of any portfolio.

Easy to Master the Principles

While we realize that Buffett, Templeton, Klarman, Gabelli, and all the other champions of value are highly intelligent, value investing does not require a brilliant mind, according to Buffett.

He suggests that beginning investors start their education by taking a class on how to buy a farm. The potential farm buyer would learn to study the property, examine the costs of running the operation, understand the income that the farm produces over time, compare its price with that of similar properties, and so forth. If the buyer can purchase the farm for less than its future worth, then he has found a bargain. He has uncovered a value investment. Now, says Buffett, substitute securities for the farm and you'll understand valuation. "Just like a farm, it is what it (the company underlying the stock or the bond) is going to produce over time."

Little Math Needed

Buffett often says he uses no other math than addition, subtraction, division, and, perhaps with wry humor, multiplication. His teacher Graham was skilled at mathematics, but had this to say about stock formulas:

> Mathematics is ordinarily considered as producing precise and dependable results; but in the stock market the more elaborate and abstruse the mathematics the more uncertain and speculative are the conclusions we draw there from.... Whenever calculus is brought in, or higher algebra, you could take it as a warning signal that the operator was trying to substitute theory for experience, and usually also to give to speculation the deceptive guise of investment.... Have no investors and security analysts eaten of the tree of knowledge of good and evil prospects? By so doing have they not permanently expelled themselves from that Eden where promising common stocks at reasonable prices could be plucked off the bushes?[3]

It has been shown fairly consistently that too much math can be a dangerous thing. When investing becomes overly technical, investors tend to place too much faith in formulas and abandon common sense. They fall prey to the "Lake Wobegon effect," which says that all the children are above average and, with such a pool of brains, what can go wrong?

It was this nearly religious faith in statistical and mathematical models that led to the credit collapse that began in 2007.

"People started to believe that the risk levels weren't so big. They relied on mathematical models that calculated exact numbers, giving them a sense of objective reality. But human interactions cannot be computed by such formulas," said Leonhard Fischer, CEO of the holding company RHJ International.[4]

"Successful investors, like successful doctors, must have a good understanding of the hard facts expressed in numbers—but then these must be applied properly to real-life cases," Irving Kahn, a protégé of Graham's and founder of the investment house Kahn Brothers, once said.[5]

"Some of the worst business decisions I've seen came with detailed analysis," noted Warren Buffett's partner Charles T. Munger. "The higher math was false precision. They do that in business schools because they've got to do *something*."[6]

Buffett followed up with a quip: "It only happens to people with high IQs."[7]

Mental Discipline Required

Nevertheless, value investing presents challenges to our human frailties for most investors. Value investing can:

- **Be counterintuitive.** Sometimes it feels like you are heading in the wrong direction. There is a close correlation between value investing and contrarian investing, although value people are not automatically contrarian.

- **Be out of step with popular thinking.** Generally current attitudes are based on short-term performance or past performance. Neither of these measures ensures superior long-term gains.

- **Lag in bull markets, especially near the top.** When you see your friends at a cocktail party and they tell you their portfolio has gained 22 percent when yours has only gained 18 percent, it is a little hard to stomach. But take comfort in the thought that your friend may have fallen victim to groupthink in regard to the stock market. The symptoms of groupthink are tendencies toward uniform thinking, overestimation of the group's ability, and closed-mindedness.[8] A crowd can artificially chase a share price higher, or in a panic pull the rug from under a share price. The question is, How safe is your friend's higher return in comparison to yours?

- **Require a reserve of cash to take advantage of investment opportunities.** During times of inflation it is tricky to stay in investments that protect against shrinking buying power and still manage to have enough cash to participate when excellent bargains appear.

- **Sometimes leave a little money on the table.** The value investor knows she probably won't buy at the absolute lowest price or sell at the highest. In fact, there is a tendency for value investors to buy and sell a little too soon, but this should not be an impediment. Don't let greed push you into higher risk activities. If you've bought at a good price and sold at a satisfactory profit, don't bemoan the loss of pennies or even a few dollars.

- **Lack the excitement of other investment approaches.** Studies show that an investor who simply bought and held an S&P 500 Index over the twenty-two years ending in 2008 would have generated an 8 percent annual gain over that period. Instead, the average investor, who typically bought individual securities at the wrong time, sold them at the wrong time, and paid transaction fees, earned just 1.9 percent.[9] But buying and holding is so darn boring.

This list of value investing vices may seem silly and easy to overcome, but that would discount the power of behavioral investing, or the influence of groupthink on all that we do. Thinking for yourself and operating outside the mainstream takes a great deal of mental strength.

Low-Maintenance Portfolio

One of the goals of value investing is to invest in a way that allows you to own a stock for a very long time. If you put together a fairly small and manageable portfolio—say fewer than thirty different stocks—and then just check in regularly to make sure you are on track, investing becomes a lot less time consuming and stressful. However, in recent years, this simple approach has become increasingly problematic.

While there are examples of its being done, buying few companies limits diversification. Also, the idea that you can profitably buy and hold any group of stocks for a lifetime may be unrealistic. It has become extremely hazardous.

"Buy and hold isn't what it used to be," wrote Whitney Tilson and John Heins in *Kiplinger's Personal Finance*. "We'd be the last to recommend frequent trading, but buying and forgetting in a world roiled by rapid change is an increasingly risky proposition, especially when it comes to technology."[10]

Tilson and Heins cite Nokia as an example. That company was king of cell phones for a while, "but as it lost a few product-cycle rounds to rivals, its descent from the throne was sharp and fast."[11]

Stable and Lasting Returns

Buffett says his favorite holding time is forever, but that attitude applies mainly to his core holdings, companies he bought at extremely low

Is Modern Portfolio Theory a Challenge to Value Investing?

Modern portfolio theory (MPT) was developed in the 1950s through the early 1970s by economist Harry Markowitz and was considered a significant advance in the mathematical modeling of finance. MPT is a combination of several arithmetic concepts, including mean-variance analysis, the capital asset pricing model, and the efficient market hypothesis mostly taught in advanced finance classes. The idea is that it is possible to build a portfolio that delivers the highest obtainable return for any given level of risk.

Another concept behind MPT is that the market is nearly impossible to beat and that the people whose returns are better than the market averages are those who take above-average risk.

Additionally MPT asserts that nobody can really beat the market over the long haul. The stock market is a zero-sum game and over time the best anyone can expect is an average performance.

The theory implies that these risk takers with higher gains will likely get clobbered when markets turn down.

Even though MPT is widely used by mutual and hedge fund managers, independent investors such as Buffett remind us that MPT, which requires detailed analysis and the use of sophisticated hedges and other techniques, hasn't been shown to work.

One example of the theory's shortcomings was the crumbling of Long-Term Capital Management beginning in 1998.

LTCM was a U.S. hedge fund that used strategies such as MPT, fixed income arbitrage, statistical arbitrage, and pairs trading, combined with high leverage. John Meriwether, the former vice chairman and head of bond trading at Salomon Brothers, founded LTCM in 1994. The fund's board of directors included many respected investors and academics.

Initially enormously successful with annualized returns of over 40 percent in its early years, LTCM lost $4.6 billion in less than four months following the Russian financial crisis of 1998.

Its collapse was spectacular, leading to a massive bailout by other major banks and investment houses that had to be supervised by the Federal Reserve. The fund folded in early 2000.

At the end of the day, MPT did not work as well in practice as it did in theory. Investment success depends on the investor's attitude, approach, and resolve. For most investors, it is wiser to pick a reasonable number of out-of-favor investments and wait for the market to recognize their worth than it is to engage in complex strategies or to rely on market averages alone.

prices. Even he exited the stock market at one point because he didn't understand why prices were so crazily high. He couldn't justify holding such issues and couldn't find anything to buy.

Buffett is known to take profits when circumstances dictate it.

Nevertheless, Graham's teachings have, over a long period of time, allowed a great many investors to maintain consistent returns of 17 percent a year and higher. This defies the idea that because the markets are a zero-sum game, nobody can beat them. True, it takes patience, persistence, and enthusiasm for the investment process. But for those who are up for the challenge, the game can be both rewarding and intriguing.

Based on historical returns, $1 million invested in value stocks after a typical five-year period would have grown to $2.2 million, compared with $1.6 million if invested in so-called glamour stocks. Over the same time period a $1 million investment in the S&P 500 Index would have grown to $1.9 million.[12]

Given an even longer period, ten years, the performance advantage of value stocks widens considerably. Over the decade the value portfolio would have grown to $4.9 million versus $3.1 million invested in glamour stocks and $3.4 million for the S&P 500 Index.[13] So while buy and hold requires attention and flexibility, it remains a target to aim for.

Chapter 4

Mr. Market

We missed the gravy, but we stayed out of the soup.
EDGAR D. "NED" JANNOTTA, CHAIRMAN, WILLIAM BLAIR & COMPANY,
DESCRIBING THE COMPANY'S PERFORMANCE DURING THE DOT-COM CRASH OF
1999–2001[1]

Watching the stock market indexes bob, weave, leap, and dive is a great spectator sport. Turn to almost any cable news outlet and you'll get a report on the latest stock market antics. "Stock prices in U.S. markets plunged today on news of a train crash in India." Or the cause may be a rumor that the U.S. president has a cold, that the British are having an extreme Atlantic storm, or there was a terrorist bombing in a former Soviet satellite country. Stock market watchers talk about the August effect (markets traditionally go down in August, perhaps because so much of Wall Street is on vacation), the October effect (before Halloween the market gets scary), and the president's effect (the market fares better after the election of a Democrat than a Republican), but no one can predict these market directions for certain. Often the so-called causes of the market bumps have little or nothing to do with investing, and in the end they are just short-term trends.

Still, we know markets are reactive. Sometimes the news prompts ordinarily sensible investors to be euphoric or to panic. This is a variation on the madness of crowds. "It's best to ignore a lot of what's going on, media discussion of what bad shape we're in. The best thing is to ignore [the babble] and keep to a long-term basic fundamental plan," said Charles Brandes.

Market Cycles

Yet by studying charts, it seems that the stock market moves in great undulating waves with smaller crests between. Charles Dow noted more than one hundred years ago that the stock market, like all of nature, moves to a tempo. The market has rhythms, and rhythms within rhythms. First there are the daily swings. The daily movements occur within longer waves lasting from thirty to forty days. The monthly vacillations morph into longer bull or bear tides lasting from four to six years.

"Nothing is more certain than that the market has three well-defined movements which fit into each other," wrote Dow.[2]

When we look closely at this sea of stocks, it is clear that each individual issue has cycles of its own. Sometimes the share price moves with the market, sometimes not. But together with other shares, it creates the swell. Just as droplets of water combine to make a mighty wave, these individual stocks move the markets. Unfortunately, the markets are not as predictable as the tides. Choppy water, storms, and even rogue waves come along.

Even seemingly serious analysts can lead us to appallingly wrong conclusions. Most securities market commentators, especially the talking heads on television, are using one of two approaches to reach their conclusions. They may be looking at past behavior patterns of the market or of a particular stock, or they may be looking forward, anticipating rates changes, estimated earnings, industry cycles, or business and political conditions that could influence corporate earnings or investor attitude. Neither point of view is scientific or a reliable indicator of future events.

Furthermore, seldom does either approach allow for a margin of safety or for adjustment to unfolding events. The information is presented as if the analyst is right or wrong and that's that.

And yet as we said earlier, the markets do seem to be cyclical. William O'Neil, founder of *Investor's Business Daily*, notes that there have been twenty-seven great market cycles since the start of record keeping in the late 1880s. "History repeats itself a lot because human nature doesn't change and the law of supply and demand doesn't change," he says. "Both are at play all the time in the market."

For the longer-term investor these market gyrations are nothing more than opportunities to buy when the price of a sound company slips and sell when shares are overvalued. Few events have instructed us more dramatically than the market implosion of 2007–8. While that episode had deep underlying causes, such as misbehavior in the credit markets and derivatives run amok, it was made worse by far too much enthusiasm when the markets were rising and excessive fear as they fell.

Mr. Market Is Volatile, but He's Also Your Friend

Ben Graham used the parable of Mr. Market to describe the best context when thinking about the stock market. Imagine, he said, that you have a business partner named Mr. Market. Mr. Market is something of a drama king, rushing around with his hair flying every which way and his clothing in disarray. He is highly emotional as he responds to one crisis after another.

Each day Mr. Market dashes into your office and offers to either buy your share or sell his share of the joint business. If things seem to be going his way he works himself into a manic state and the price he sets for the business goes higher and higher. If he is depressed about something, the price withers with his mood. As distracting as his antics may be, you can count on Mr. Market to keep showing up, day after day, with a price. This partner does not drive the stock market, he *is* the stock market, and he is there so that you can invest and divest as you please.

"Human nature, psychology, supply and demand doesn't change," William O'Neil reemphasizes. "People keep piling in on the way up, piling out on the way down."

To say that value investors do not get caught up in market histrionics is not to say that we ignore market swings altogether. Graham advised investors to remain calm and consider Mr. Market's offer in light of all the available facts.

"The investor's primary interest lies in acquiring and holding suitable securities at suitable prices. Market movements are important to him in a practical sense because they alternately create low price levels at which he would be wise to buy and high price levels at which he certainly should refrain from buying and probably would be wise to sell," wrote Graham.[3]

It is safe for the investor to make two assumptions:

- Quite often the market is out of step with true value. Sometimes the misalignment is a canyon; at other times it is a crevice.

- Sooner or later the market will correct and even overcorrect itself. Stocks that are under- or overpriced tend to adjust in the direction of intrinsic value.

Timing Compared with Pricing

There are two ways of dealing with a market that is always moving in one direction or the other. You can time the market or you can price it.

The market timer attempts to predict the future direction of the market, typically by using technical indicators or economic data. The timer is looking for market bottoms where he will buy stocks or peaks where he will sell and take profits. The timer may also switch among mutual fund asset classes in an effort to profit from the changes in their market outlook.

The Pricing Approach

As the name suggests, those who price the market buy when the price of an individual security is right. Market pricing is primarily determined by the interaction of supply and demand. A high demand for a stock drives the price higher; prices fall when demand falls. Contrarian and value investors price the market, partly because the stocks they prefer become unpopular now and then.

Since he considered timing well nigh impossible, Graham exploited market behavior by buying and selling on the basis of price. He bought stocks when prices had declined and securities were undervalued. He sold when prices vaulted above the intrinsic value of the stock or bond. In the majority of cases this practice will find the value investor acting ahead of market swings rather than after them.

Futility of Market Timing

Charles Dow wrote in a 1902 column, "In dealing with the stock market there is no way of telling when the top of an advance or the bottom of a decline has been reached until some time after such top or bottom has been made. Sometimes people are able to guess when prices are at the top or bottom, but such guesses are of their nature not of particular value, and it is a proverb in Wall Street, that only a foolish speculator hopes to buy stocks at the lowest and sell them at the highest. The speculator with experience knows that no one can do this with certainty or regularity."[4]

Always Amazed

According to value investor and fund manager Charles Brandes: "I've always said and say it even now, value investors— any investors—will continue to be amazed at the short-term market fluctuations and economy fluctuations. No matter how much you anticipate how much a stock price could go or how high it could go, it will always do more. Even value investors like myself can be amazed at how fluctuations in prices will happen. I see no change in that at all."

Buffett says that market timing is a huge temptation for most investors. He often observes what he calls the Cinderella Syndrome. "They (investors) go to the ball, knowing the pumpkin is going to turn at midnight, but everyone thinks they'll leave at five minutes to twelve. No way that can happen."

"As a pure value investor, you're not going to pick the tops," concurs David Iben, manager of the $574 million Nuveen Tradewinds Value Opportunities Fund. Iben considers himself a contrarian who seeks out deep value. Iben earned investors an average return of more than 17 percent in the three years preceding the 2007–8 crash. In 2008 his portfolio was off 32 percent, then in 2009 it rebounded just over 40 percent.

The Opposite of Day Trading

There is a surge of excitement and a curtain of shadow surrounding day trading—the popular practice of profiting from quick trades in and out of securities as the market fluctuates. By its very definition, day trading is the ultimate test of market timing. As the sophistication of personal computers has exploded, so has fascination with day trading.

There are hundreds of organizations appealing to the gambling instinct in most of us by marketing the idea that you can sit at home all day in your pajamas and earn a fabulous living as a day trader. The pitchmen are making great money providing training, software, and support, which in some cases can cost as much as $45,000.

Nobody knows for sure how many day traders there are because often it is done anonymously and privately. There is a small cadre of professional day traders who work for investment firms, but even in that group, life moves fast and careers are sometimes short. Research has shown that those using software at home are likely to be much less successful than other investors.[5] Numerous studies have shown that approximately 70 percent of day traders lose money, and that most operate in a way that puts 100 percent of their capital at risk.[6] When they lose, they often lose their entire investment cache.

Potential day traders, like all investors, must take into consideration all the expenses involved in their work, including taxes and the cost of lost opportunities.

The Investor Home Web site explains how all of these elements work together. "For instance, let's say day trader Loren has $125,000 in capital, currently makes $100,000 a year, and quits the job to start day trading. Loren expects to use $25,000 for living expenses for the next six months and the remaining $100,000 for risk capital. At the end of six months Loren has lost half the capital and is left with $50,000. How much is Loren out from making the decision to day trade? The answer is *not* $50,000."[7]

In addition to the day trading loss of $50,000, Loren is out the $50,000 income from the former job, plus gains from the $50,000 had it been invested in a way that preserved principal and either collected interest or allowed it to appreciate.

Some day traders come out of it worse than Loren. Many rely on borrowed money, such as buying stocks on margin, to leverage their wins. When their account goes in the red, they also can end up deep in personal debt.

Day trading is a highly hazardous activity; it requires enormous time and energy; it is stressful, and even when there are gains, traders seldom earn a greater return than they would by simply acquiring good, underpriced companies and holding them quietly until they reach or exceed their true value.

Buffett doesn't approve of frequent trading, even when it is not at the speed or velocity of traditional day trading. "We believe that according the name 'investors' to institutions that trade actively is like calling someone who repeatedly engages in one-night stands a 'romantic.'"

"People think they can dance in and out of the market," says Buffett, "making money off other people, but the business is risky." But most traders can't resist one last dance and end up getting clocked.

"That said, I suspect if you have the temperament of a day trader, one who is highly competitive and enjoys the thrill of risk, this is the path you will choose," Buffett continued. "But for those who prefer less stress, not to worry. You are likely to make more money with value investing, and you are less likely to lose your poker stake."

"For the typical retail investor," said securities attorney Philip A. Feigin, "day trading isn't investing. It's gambling. If you want to gamble, go to Las Vegas; the food is better."[8]

High-Speed Trading

In recent years many hedge funds and institutional traders have developed computer programs that execute buy and sell orders in milliseconds. For some institutions, flash trading is a way of staying competitive.

They trade in large volumes where a savings of pennies per share makes a difference.

However, there is a brand of hedge funds that uses sophisticated systems to arbitrage large numbers of shares, making profits on very small price spreads. Some high-speed funds make thousands of trades a second and hold the shares for a matter of minutes. These high-frequency trades now make up 61 percent of the more than 10 billion shares traded daily on the various U.S. exchanges.[9]

Those engaging in this type of trading claim that it increases liquidity for all investors. The critics worry that because the trades are so large, often running into billions of dollars, and are so fast, an error or a miscalculation could cause catastrophic damage to the U.S. and world economies. Something like this happened in 1987 when, due to extensive use of automated stop loss orders, the market plummeted 22 percent in a single day.

For most investors, however, a penny or two a share does not significantly affect returns. And since these trades usually are not based on market fundamentals, they give the market motion, but do not permanently drive markets in one direction or another.

Watching a Bull Run

In early 2007 the stock market exhibited the classic characteristics of an overheated, charging market:

- Share prices were historically high.

- Price-to-earnings ratios soared.

- Dividend yields were low compared with bond yields and compared with their own normal dividend yield patterns.

- Margin buying became excessive as investors rushed to leverage their gains to even higher levels.

Quite often when the market is torrid there is a swarm of new stock offerings, especially those either of questionable quality or of companies so young they have not yet become profitable. A bull market presents a window of initial public offering (IPO) opportunity because optimistic investors expect and are willing to fork over high prices for new issues.

The Pinnacle of the Bull Market

As explained earlier, no one can tell for sure when the market hits a top. Like the beginning and ending of recessions, you only know for certain when looking in a rearview mirror.

"Bull market tops tend to be long and drawn out with first one group, then the next group fading away," explains Richard Russell of the Dow Theory Letters.[10]

Even so, at the apex the roller coaster often pauses and shudders, causing great jerking motions in the markets.

At this point, there are only two reasonable strategies:

- If you haven't already reduced its size, sell off your portfolio; stash the profits in a safe place and wait for the market to cool off. When stock market prices decline to where your investments again have a margin of safety, it is time to return to buying. This sounds easy enough, but many investors simply cannot sell shares when the price is rising. Others are so focused on the tax consequences of their sale that they hesitate to sell. In both cases the danger is dithering until the price has declined to the point that there are no longer profits or tax consequences.

- The second possible game plan is to sell only those stocks that are out of breath and clearly overvalued. Stick with those companies that still have the energy for a long-distance run. Then when the market normalizes, begin refilling the vacancies in your portfolio with bargain issues.

Both strategies require resolve, discipline, and patience.

Falling Back to Normal Territory

Charles Brandes reminds us that the 2007–8 calamity all started with the collapse of the subprime mortgage market and spread to other credit areas. While the signs were there, Brandes said he himself didn't get the timing right because he failed to anticipate the magnitude of the problem. "I think we saw it to a large extent, but not totally," said Brandes. "You could see some very obvious, stupid things happening. I was looking in 2005 and 2006 at real estate, when it was starting to be ridiculous. But everyone had the assumption—bankers and mortgage people—that real estate would either hold its value or keep going up. I thought it was ridiculous back then and got out. We backed off from bank stocks and wouldn't touch mortgages. My timing was off. It all kept going up. We were early, as value people always are."

Pulling Bargains from the Rubble

"Generally," said Brandes, "it's a mistake for investors to try to time the market; on the other hand, you've got to become more cautious when you see things like this happening in the real estate market. It just takes a tremendous amount of patience. Human beings don't have a lot of long-term patience."

The Brandes letter to investors at the end of 2008 talked about all the extreme value investments that by then had become available. The prices of thousands of solid companies such as Google, Apple, BP, and Toyota were battered and cheap.

While that short period of extreme values passed within a year, some excellent stocks remained well priced for quite some time. Brandes explained there were many opportunities for those who were patient, who focused on long-term earnings and did not worry about market fluctuations and who were willing to invest globally. Brandes looked to temporarily out-of-favor industries that are fundamental to life and the economy, such as pharmaceuticals and telecommunications, to add strength and sustainable growth to his various investment funds.

"Banks are an example. It is a necessity to have banks and to lend money, a necessity. If you look out three to five years on earnings, you can see a lot of bargains today." And yet, said Brandes, you must be realistic when analyzing bank stocks. "Banks probably will not be as leveraged in the future and they will be required to add to their capital strength, which is a good thing, but which also will reduce rates of return."

His advice applied to banks at that phase of the economic cycle, but at any given time, looking forward is useful. Making exact predictions of future events and the timing of those events isn't possible, but common sense will lead investors in the right direction. We can learn from history and not be doomed to repeat it.

The Behavior of a Bear

The floor of the bear's den is no easier to find than is the top of a bull market. As share prices descend deeper and deeper, the pundits ask again and again, is this the bottom? Some even bravely announce what they see as the bottom.

There are signs, of course. The market indices are at or near record lows. There is quantitative evidence in the corporate balance sheets, income statements, price-to-earnings ratios, dividend yields, and other numbers.

Investors tend to be in a dark mood and are unwilling to reenter the stock market, no matter how enticing prices may be.

Dividend Yield

The dividend yield, the percentage of a company's dividend in relation to its share price, has been a fairly reliable measure of investment cycles for many decades. The dividend yield theory of investing uses the concept that for companies with a long dividend record, it is often possible to determine if the share price is overvalued or undervalued by studying the dividend pattern. When the stock is overselling at too high of a price, the dividend yield will be historically low. When the share price falls, the dividend yield increases. For example, if a stock is selling at $100 and every year pays a $5 dividend, the dividend yield is 5 percent. If the share price goes to $200, the dividend yield drops to 2.5 percent. However, if the share price falls to $50, the yield rises to 10 percent. As long as the company is on reasonably sound footing otherwise, it becomes a better buy as the price falls and the dividend increases. Certain old companies have a predictable dividend cycle that some investors use to guide their purchases and sales.

The dividend yield on the Dow Jones Industrial Average, as is the case with individual issues, moves inversely to share prices. Typically the Dow swings between a high yield of 6 percent at the bottom of the market and a low yield of 3 percent at the height. With the exception of the years between 1994 and 2007, a rising price trend has reversed when the dividend yield shrank to below 3 percent. The Dow's average dividend yield sometimes stretches beyond these points, and each dividend-paying stock has its own cyclical history, but still, this is a telling phenomenon. During these aberrant years the market continued on for quite a while with a historically low dividend yield, so when the reversal came, it was sudden and severe.

Many companies restrict dividends when earnings are low but increase them as the outlook improves, so a rising dividend is an indication of an increasingly confident company. Unfortunately, dividends usually go out of fashion during a bull market, as investors prefer a rising share price to dividend income. Many young and rapidly growing companies plow profits back into the enterprise, as they should do. In these cases there is no dividend history to turn to.

By mid-2008, when the market was bottoming out, there were many stocks with exciting dividend yields. Of the companies listed on U.S. stock exchanges that pay dividends, more than 1,200—over 40 percent—had yields above 5 percent. At that time the yield on a Treasury bill was less than 4 percent. McGraw-Hill, hit by trouble in its ratings service, was one of those companies with a 5 percent dividend. Within a year, however, the share price increased and the dividend yield receded to 2.8 percent.

While a healthy dividend yield is one clue to intrinsic value, and while the dividend can present a margin of safety, even the dividend gauge must be checked against other data. To confirm the safety of the dividend, look for companies with little debt, comfortable cash reserves, and growing revenue and income.

The subject of dividends will come up again in chapter 10.

Time to Invest Again, but the Trust Is Gone

When the share prices are trading at values affording a nice margin of safety, there should be joy in the streets. Buffett says during these times he is so happy he tap-dances to work every day.

Buffett explained to his shareholders that in 2008, "disarray in markets gave us a tailwind in our purchases. When investing, pessimism is your friend, euphoria the enemy. In our insurance portfolios, we made three large investments on terms that would be unavailable in normal markets."

However, at times like these investors can be so traumatized by what they've been through that they hang back. Writer and investor James Grant once said, "In almost every other walk of life, people buy more at lower prices; in the stock and bond market they seem to buy more at higher prices."[11]

Be Cheerful When Mr. Market Is Blue

Writing in *The New York Times* in October of 2008, Buffett tried to encourage others to return to the stock market. Buffett wrote that in his personal account, he had started buying American stocks. Why? "Be fearful when others are greedy, and be greedy when others are fearful," he advised. "And most certainly, fear is now widespread, gripping even seasoned investors. To be sure, investors are right to be wary of highly leveraged entities or businesses in weak competitive positions. But fears regarding the long-term prosperity of the nation's many sound companies make no sense. These businesses will indeed suffer earnings hiccups, as they always have. But most major companies will be setting new profit records in 10 and 20 years from now."[12]

Buffett also admitted that he might have been acting ahead of the markets, that his new purchases may languish before they rise in price, but it is almost impossible to know when the market will turn. The time to act is when you see bargains: ". . . if you wait for robins, spring will be over."[13]

David Iben says that "it is usually better to be too early than too late. This is true even when early turns out to be painful."[14]

Buffett stresses the importance of staying calm as markets go crazy. You should stay your own course. "If you owned a group of good companies a few years ago, you were fine two years ago and you're fine now. You don't want to let your investment decision be ruined by collected errors of others," says Buffett.

Charles Brandes tells his clients, "Investing is not only about staying disciplined, but critically reexamining investment decisions."[15]

The Biography of GEICO

The story of the Government Employees Insurance Co. is an example of capitalism working well. It shows how the shares of one of the greatest investments ever can fluctuate and present—more than once—enticing opportunities for disciplined value investors such as Warren Buffett.

GEICO was launched during the Great Depression by Texans Leo Goodwin and his wife Lillian. Leo had been an accountant for an insurance company, and believed he could build a low-risk automobile insurance company by selling directly to government employees. Government workers, he noticed, had fewer accidents, paid their bills, and were safe to insure. The Goodwins started with $100,000 capital, 75 percent of it coming from Fort Worth banker Cleaves Rhea. The company was born in 1936 in Texas, and a year later moved to Washington, D.C. Within four years the company was profitable.

In 1948 the Rhea family decided to sell most of its interest, but had no luck shopping the family-owned company around Wall Street. When a representative called on the Graham Newman Co. that changed. Benjamin Graham recognized GEICO's value instantly, although he also saw areas of risk. He would have liked the assets to be stronger, but most of all, he felt that the acquisition required a bit too much of Graham Newman's resources. Conservative Graham quaked at the idea of sinking 25 percent of his firm's assets into any single investment.

Graham overcame his doubts and paid $720,000 for a majority of GEICO, which incidentally represented the same percentage of the company for which Buffett in 1995 would pay $2.3 billion.

Indeed Graham had made a mistake, although not a financial one. At the time an investment company could not own more than 10 percent of an insurance company. The Securities and Exchange Commission demanded that Graham rescind the sale. The sellers refused to take the company back, so Graham worked out a deal with the SEC. He would spin off GEICO and distribute the shares to investors in the Graham Newman Fund.

Soon afterward GEICO went public on the New York Stock Exchange at $27 per share. The company later spun off several subsidiaries to investors and the stock split numerous times. It is estimated that between 1948 and 1972 the shares appreciated more than 28,000 percent.

In the early 1970s Graham and his partner Jerry Newman decided to retire from the GEICO board. Graham nominated Warren Buffett to replace him, but Buffett was rejected because the board felt his other insurance holdings presented a conflict of interest. Not a good decision, as it turned out.

Buffett had taken a special interest in insurance companies when he was studying under Graham at Columbia. In 1951 Buffett jumped on a train to Washington, D.C., to visit the company, beginning his education in risk and the insurance world. He put insurance at the center of what he calls his "circle of competence." Buffett invested

65 percent of his net worth in GEICO, $7,000 at the time. He later sold those shares at their peak price.

In 1973 GEICO shares were trading at around $60, but they plunged to $5 by 1976. The founders' son, who was running the company, committed suicide.

Seeing his second opportunity, Buffett again invested in GEICO, buying 1.3 million shares at an average cost of $3.18 per share. By stages, Buffett increased his position until he owned 51 percent of the insurer. In 1996, Buffett's company, Berkshire Hathaway, purchased the remainder of GEICO at slightly below book value.

In 1995 GEICO was the United States' sixth largest auto insurer and by 2010 it had climbed to number three. Over the same period of time GEICO's float grew from $2.7 billion to $9.6 billion. "Equally important," said Buffett, "GEICO has operated at an underwriting profit in 13 of the 14 years Berkshire has owned it."[16]

Chapter 5

Risk Versus Reward

The natural tendency in times like these is to avoid risk. We are seeking to
rationally balance risk and potential return.

BRANDES INVESTMENT PARTNERS

There are dozens of theories for determining what degree of investment risk is appropriate to take at specific income levels, various ages, and a multitude of circumstances. Internet sites offer intriguing calculators for determining the exact percentage or dollar amount to put into stocks for any special circumstance. There are betas for almost everything. While these calculations are helpful in that they give us some sense of direction, they also can be a hindrance to the extent that they mask good common sense.

Balancing Risk

One of the greatest lessons of the twenty-first century—so far—is that we all should aim for a healthy balance in our financial lives. Stock market investing is for those who have solid financial footing, a reasonable mortgage, who can pay off their credit cards each month, and who have at least six months' living expenses in a reasonably liquid account such as a savings account, money market fund, or short-term certificate of deposit. Additionally, you should have stashed as much money as allowed in a tax-advantaged account such as your company 401(k), an individual retirement account, or a Roth IRA.

And another thing: "... let me be very clear," says the ubiquitous financial adviser Suze Orman. "I have always said invest in the [stock] market only with money that you do not need for at least 10 years or longer, preferably longer."[1] That may be extraordinarily conservative advice, but it has merit. Remember how quickly the housing market collapsed and the stock market tumbled right behind it? And woe to those who lost their jobs soon afterward.

Americans had enjoyed reasonably calm markets for such a long time that we forgot the need to protect ourselves, even if it meant a smaller home, less exotic vacations, and lower overall investment returns. Warren Buffett often warns us that the first rule of finance is to not lose money, and the second rule is to remember the first rule. His words apply to all aspects of personal finances, not just to the stock market.

What We Know About Risk

We understand certain things about risk instinctually. In general, younger people can take more risk than older folk; they have time to adjust their investment style and earn back losses. Those with small incomes and lower savings accounts can handle less risk than those who have abundant current income, little debt, and an overflowing rainy-day fund. The sooner you need to use your investment money, the more conservative you should become.

We also realize that while mathematics is a great tool, it can lead to overconfidence. Nothing illustrates this more than Wall Street's love affair with quantitative analysis, and specifically the famous "Gaussian copula function," which *Wired* magazine called "the formula that killed Wall Street."

The GCF formula was the brainchild of a bright Canadian-educated Chinese economist named David X. Li. In 2000 Li published a paper in *The Journal of Fixed Income* under the title "On Default Correlation: A Copula Function Approach." Li's formula was a simple, elegant method of calculating risk that quickly caught fire and swept from bond investors to big banks, hedge funds, traders, rating agencies, and even regulators. The formula was used to measure the risk of mortgage-backed securities, and gave those working in the industry the confidence to bundle trillions of dollars of loans, bonds, or whatever asset they had into collateralized debt obligations. The problem was that the formula was untested in the real world and was based on analysis of highly volatile and unstable financial instruments.

Many economists, including Li himself, warned that there were risks associated with the Gaussian copula function, but few people listened. After all, the formula seemed smart and did its work inside a computer, which wrapped it in the slick packaging of modernity and technology.

"Li can't be blamed," said Kai Gilkes of the credit research firm CreditSights. "After all, he just invented the model. Instead, we should blame the bankers who misinterpreted it. And even then, the real danger was created not because any given trader adopted it but because every trader did. In financial markets, everybody doing the same thing is the classic recipe for a bubble and inevitable bust."[2]

When housing prices tumbled, unemployment began rising and defaults of all kind spread, trillions of dollars turned to cinders, and the world financial system nearly burned down. The moral of the story? It is the same for professional investors as it is for everyone else. Don't get involved in any approach or form of investing you don't completely understand. Risk is inherent in all financial activity. It is unavoidable, but you can prepare for it, guard against it, and minimize it. In this process, practical thinking goes a long way.

The Correlation Between Risk and Reward

"Sometimes risk and reward are correlated in a positive fashion . . . the exact opposite is true in value investing. If you buy a dollar for 60 cents, it is riskier than if you buy a dollar for 40 cents, but the expectation for reward is greater in the latter case," Graham told us.

That reasoning brings us back to Graham's concept of a "margin of safety," which Buffett insists does not require higher math. Simply put, the margin of safety is the difference between an estimate of an asset's underlying fundamental value and its share price. When dealing in stocks, if the spread goes into negative numbers, the company's shares are overvalued. At times the difference between these two figures will be narrow. At other times it will be broad, and that is the condition we're looking for.

To quote David Iben, "We're still suckers for big discounts to book value. We like the downside protection and staying power that book value often provides."[3]

To ensure a margin of safety, look for a substantial excess of value in some area. That margin may be provided by great reserves of an essential commodity, a new product that is a leader in its field, or strong cash holdings. Additionally, try to:

- Buy when stock markets are in a down cycle and there are many undervalued issues. This was the case in late 2008 and early 2009.

- Look for companies under temporary stress. Investors who had the insight to evaluate and to buy leading banks following the crash of 2007–8 found great bargains. In late 2009 Toyota began a recall of certain vehicles due to a deadly, sticky accelerator. The problem gained momentum and by early 2010 the company recalled more than eight million vehicles, a costly episode that seriously damaged its formerly excellent reputation. Toyota's stock traded at 91.78 on January 19, 2010, but once investors realized the seriousness of the situation the stock began to tumble. It traded as low as 68 but by mid-2010 seemed to be stabilizing. It looked for a while as if Toyota was done for. However, both Ford and General Motors had experienced similar recalls earlier in their histories and their stock eventually recovered. Value investors were watching Toyota and evaluating it as a deep value for those with the patience to wait for recovery.

- Scour the exchanges for overlooked stocks even when the market is not in a bearish mood.

Informed Speculation

In his book *Margin of Safety,* Seth Klarman divided assets and securities into two classes—investments and speculations. Investments, he said, "throw off cash for the benefit of owners; speculations do not."

Graham defined speculation somewhat differently. He considered it a higher or extraordinary level of risk. He often said that speculation is acceptable as long as it is *informed* speculation. By that he meant that the investor must be well aware of the risk involved, must have been diligent in his research, and must have good reason to believe that the level of potential profits compensates for the greater level of risk.

How Beta Works

Market risk and volatility of investing in stocks is commonly measured by a factor called beta. Beta was designed to help investors make choices regarding the type of investment that best suits their risk tolerance.

The beta coefficient is a key parameter in the capital asset pricing model (CAPM). It is estimated for individual companies using regression analysis to produce a quantitative measure of the volatility of a specific stock, mutual fund, or portfolio, relative to the overall market, usually the S&P 500. It indicates the performance that particular investment vehicle has experienced in the past five years as the S&P moved 1 percent up or down. A beta above 1 is more volatile than the overall market, while a beta below 1 is less volatile.

If the stock moves exactly as the market does, its beta will be 1. When you see a negative beta, it means that the stock goes down every time the market goes up.

A stock that goes up 20 percent while the index appreciates by 10 percent will have a beta of 2, while a stock with beta 1.2 means that the stock should go up 20 percent more than the index.

For example, if the fictitious Also-Ran Company has a beta value of 0.70, it indicates that the potential return of the company's stock is equal to 70 percent of that of the market as a whole. By comparison, if the also made-up Bright Company has a beta value of 1.30, this means that it will potentially give a return of 30 percent more than the overall market.

Higher-beta stocks are considered to be riskier, but in turn are supposed to present a potential for higher returns. Penny stocks tend to have very high betas. Conversely, low-beta stocks pose less risk offset by lower returns. Old, established companies often exhibit low betas.

Beta, as you might expect, can also be zero. Some zero-beta assets are considered to be risk-free, such as Treasury bonds and cash. But a zero beta does not necessarily mean free of risk; a beta can be zero simply because there is no correlation between that investment vehicle and the market. An example would be betting on dog races. The correlation between the stock market and dog racing will be zero, but betting on dogs certainly is not a risk-free activity.

Companies that produce consumer goods and necessities, such as food companies and public utilities, tend to have low betas. They are less affected by changes in the economy. Those that produce or sell luxury items and durable goods have higher betas because people can choose not to buy the products when money is tight. A high debt level can also elevate a company's beta.

Yet beta doesn't always accurately reflect investment risk. One reason is that betas tend to be unstable. Also, the numbers used to calculate beta are backward-looking, or based on historical data. Relying too heavily on beta information can lead to disappointing results.

Beta and Risk

While Buffett agrees that beta can be helpful as an indicator of volatility, he often points out that greater volatility does not measure risk or necessarily correlate to higher returns.

Money manager Bruce Grantier says, "... a body of research has emerged which challenges the theory. Value stocks, those with low price/earnings ratios (P/Es) and low price/book ratios (P/Bs) were found to have lower *betas* but have *higher historical* returns than growth stocks. This was contrary to the notion that returns go hand in hand with risk, which is at the heart of MPT."[4]

Seth Klarman of The Baupost Group holds a similar view. "I find it preposterous that a single number reflecting past price fluctuations could be thought to completely describe the risk in a security," wrote Klarman.[5]

Beta, he says, has several weaknesses as a measure of risk:

- It views risk solely from the perspective of market prices, failing to take into consideration specific business fundamentals or economic developments.

- The price level is ignored, as if IBM selling at $50 per share would not be a lower-risk investment than the same IBM at $100 per share.

- Beta fails to consider the influence that investors themselves can exert on the riskiness of their holdings through such efforts as proxy contests, shareholder resolutions, communications with management, or the ultimate purchase of enough stock to gain corporate control and, with it, direct influence on underlying value.

- Beta also assumes that the upside potential and downside risk of any investment are basically equal, being simply a function of that investment's volatility compared with that of the market as a whole.

"This too is inconsistent with the world as we know it," says Klarman. "The reality is that past security price volatility does not reliably predict future investment performance (or even future volatility) and therefore is a poor measure of risk."[6]

Charles Brandes agrees. "Volatility is measurable, uncertainty is not . . . defining volatility as risk (as MPT does) obscures the true definition of investment risk as the possibility of losing money," says Brandes.

"Beta is used primarily by those who are looking at the whole market (or large numbers of stocks within it) and who don't look in detail at the fundamentals of specific companies. As I have shown for value investors, this concept is irrelevant and downright dangerous at worst."[7]

Buffett often uses his investment in the Washington Post Company to show how risk works:

"The Washington Post Company in 1973 was selling for $80 million in the market," Graham once explained. "At that time . . . the assets were worth $400 million, probably more. Now if the stock had declined even further to a price that made the valuation $40 million instead of $80 million, its beta would have been greater. And to people who think beta measures risk, the cheaper price would have made it look riskier. This is truly 'Alice in Wonderland [thinking].' "[8]

While beta is an interesting and informative aspect of investing, following it slavishly can be illogical.

Know What Kind of Investor You Are—Active or Passive

Any kind of investing takes time, temperament, and knowledge, and it all starts with self-knowledge.

Graham called an active investor an "enterprising" one. This person has the interest and ability, including the time and dedication, to manage his or her own investments.

The passive investor may have equal ability, but less interest in or time for studying stocks and bonds. Graham saw the passive investor as one who should be "defensive." This investor is best off buying broad index funds of the stock market, such as the S&P 500, and bond funds. For further diversification, this investor might divide investments between a Dow Jones Index and the S&P. However, straying into exchange traded funds (ETFs) or indexes covering only certain segments of the market would easily move the passive investor into an area of elevated risk. Both Graham and Buffett distinguish between an investor and a thrill-seeker who gambles in the securities markets.

For the Passive Investor:
Mutual Funds and Other Investment Pools

John Bogle, founder of the $1.24 trillion Vanguard group of mutual funds, has been a pioneer and innovator in the mutual fund business. Yet in 2009 Bogle severely rebuked the industry in which he has worked for nearly forty years. Mutual funds have been one of the most important tools of a passive investor, but Bogle called for deep reforms that would help individual investors and the economy as a whole.

In the past fifty years, noted Bogle, "Ownership of U.S. stocks by institutions . . . has soared more than seven times over—from 8 percent of shares all those years ago to more than 70 percent today. But in our new 'agency society,' with financial intermediaries as a group now holding clear voting control of corporate America, our agents have failed to behave as owners. Indeed, in far too many cases, they have placed their own interests ahead of the interest of their *principals*, largely those 100 million families who are the owners of our mutual funds and the beneficiaries of our pension plans." [9]

As a result a number of abuses have arisen, including focus on short-term speculation, failure to exercise adequate due diligence in research and analysis, soaring fund expenses, and over-the-top spending on advertising, including almost half a billion dollars between 2007 and 2009. So, as Bogle notes, even mutual funds don't offer the safety and rewards that investors have been promised and have the right to expect.

Bogle has called for federal regulations requiring money managers to have a greater fiduciary responsibility to their clients. Financial legislation passed in 2010 addresses some of these issues, although the level of enforcement remains to be seen.

Although overall mutual funds are as risky as stocks, there are exceptions. Many, including value-based mutual funds, have been sound investments. First Wilshire Securities is one example: a composite of First Wilshire's various portfolios earned a net annualized 20.3 percent return between 2000 and 2010, compared with 3.5 percent for the Russell 2000. The T. Rowe Price Small-Cap Value mutual fund has returned a net annualized 11.9 percent for nearly twenty years.[10]

Index Funds

Bogle is credited with creating the first index fund in 1988, thus launching a whole new industry, so it's no wonder that he has considered these low-cost funds to be a passive investor's best friend. And he's not alone in this view.

Buffett says, "The small investor should buy index funds over time. By doing this you avoid buying shares at the wrong time. It is a low-cost way of being in the market for those who don't want to do the work. The big danger is doing the wrong thing. If you don't do the wrong thing you stand a good chance of doing something reasonably right."

The most effective index fund for broad U.S. markets is one that follows the Standard & Poor's 500 Index, considered the leading benchmark for U.S. equity performance. The S&P 500 consists of the five hundred most widely held companies representing a range of industries. The S&P Index Committee chooses the stocks, following the guideline, "leading companies in leading industries."

Charles T. Munger, Buffett's longtime partner, often says that the funds of not-for-profit organizations, university endowments, and other such organizations nearly always should be invested in low-cost index

Mimicking the Dow

It would be impossible for an individual or small investor to build an index fund mimicking something as large as the S&P 500 or other specialty indexes. However, with only thirty stocks, the Dow Jones Industrial Average can be replicated, at least to a large extent. It would be difficult to exactly match the Dow's performance, since the stocks in the index are weighted according to size and other factors. Nevertheless, an investor could get close to the same returns by purchasing equal dollar amounts of the Dow component stocks listed here.

Company	Symbol	Industry
3M	MMM	Conglomerate
Alcoa	AA	Aluminum
American Express	AXP	Consumer finance
AT&T	T	Telecommunication
Bank of America	BAC	Banking
Boeing	BA	Aerospace & defense
Caterpillar	CAT	Construction & mining equipment
Chevron Corporation	CVX	Oil & gas
Cisco Systems	CSCO	Computer networking
Coca-Cola	KO	Beverages
DuPont	DD	Chemical industry
ExxonMobil	XOM	Oil & gas

General Electric	GE	Conglomerate
Hewlett-Packard	HPQ	Technology
Home Depot	HD	Home improvement retailer
IBM	IBM	Computer technology
Intel	INTC	Semiconductors
Johnson & Johnson	JNJ	Pharmaceuticals
JPMorgan Chase	JPM	Banking
Kraft Foods	KFT	Food processing
McDonald's	MCD	Fast food
Merck	MRK	Pharmaceuticals
Microsoft	MSFT	Software
Pfizer	PFE	Pharmaceuticals
Procter & Gamble	PG	Consumer goods
Travelers	TRV	Insurance
United Technologies Corp.	UTX	Conglomerate
Verizon Communications	VZ	Telecommunication
Wal-Mart	WMT	Retail
Walt Disney	DIS	Broadcasting & entertainment

funds. By following this strategy boards of directors could save a lot of time and money for their contributors. When the fees of professional money managers are taken into consideration, along with performances near or only slightly better than benchmark indexes, these organizations would invest less time and energy and fare better.

Exchange Traded Funds

In the past decade exchange traded funds have far outstripped the popularity of classic index funds. ETFs are index funds that can be bought and sold through a broker in the financial markets. Regular index funds, on the other hand, are bought in the same way that mutual funds are. There are currently about 1,500 ETFs traded on various U.S. exchanges.

Sometimes an ETF is a sampling of the entire index, but often they are constructed of some specialized aspect of the securities market. An ETF may represent, for example, oil stocks, currencies, or gold mining shares.

ETFs can be trustworthy competitors to their ancestor the index fund if they offer a low expense ratio and high tax efficiency, and if they are purchased and held for the long term.

ETFs, however, have a slippery side. John Bogle warns that it is all too easy to turn ETFs into gambling chips. When they are traded on a short-term basis, often in an attempt to game the markets, Bogle says, they "can only be described as short-term speculation."[11]

"These nouveau index funds starkly contradict each of the principal concepts underlying the original index fund," writes Bogle. "If the broadest possible diversification was the original paradigm, surely holding small segments of the market offers less diversification and commensurately more risk. If the original paradigm was minimal cost, then holding market-sector index funds that may themselves be low-cost obviates neither the brokerage commissions entailed in trading them nor the tax burdens incurred if one has the good fortune to do so successfully."[12] In other words, frequent trading both runs up the cost and increases taxes, just as day trading so often does.

Is Program Trading Your Enemy?

Program trading, which has been in use since the 1970s, has earned a shady reputation. The very words sometimes make investors fearful. Program trading is the simultaneous buying or selling of a group of stocks, as opposed to trading just one stock at a time. Most often this is done electronically in large lots by major trading houses. The aggregate of program trading constitutes somewhere between 10 percent and 45 percent of the trading volume on the New York Stock Exchange each day, and should be of little direct concern to value investors. Usually, program trading involves shares traded on one of the leading exchanges and their corresponding options traded on other exchanges. These securities are bought and sold based purely on their price in relation to one another on a predetermined basis.

In the 1980s, when program trading was relatively new, it caught the blame whenever stock prices moved quickly, especially if they went down. Many investors suspected that program trading triggered, or at least intensified, the October 1987 market crash. In subsequent years research has shown that fear of program trading has been overblown. For those buying, holding for the long term, and selling on a value basis, program trading is just one of the elements creating an active market, which in turn creates opportunities to buy or sell at a desired price.

A Word About Derivatives

A derivative is any financial instrument that is based on, or built around, some other asset, such as stocks, bonds, or indexes. Futures and options are the oldest and most familiar derivatives, although over time many derivatives have become incredibly convoluted. While most individual investors don't put their money in complicated derivatives, these financial instruments do show up in hedge and other funds and on the balance sheets of companies that we may wish to evaluate.

To make a broad, sweeping statement, derivatives can be treacherous. Experienced investors use sophisticated formulas, such as the Black-Scholes formula, to determine the risk of these complex and mysterious instruments. But even their refined tools do not always save them.

"Indeed, recent events demonstrate that certain big name CEOs (or former CEOs) were simply incapable of managing a business with a huge, complex book of derivatives," writes Buffett. "Include Charlie and me in this hapless group."[13]

While Buffett still maintains a comparatively moderate book of derivatives he found that were selling cheap, generally he steers clear of them. He learned this lesson after acquiring the British insurance giant General Re in 1998. Once he realized the huge number of precarious derivatives General Re held he closed down the company's derivatives section at a loss of $400 million rather than continuing to carry the onerous, long-term risk. The closing was a prolonged and painful process.

Greater transparency as provided by new laws, Buffett says, will not make derivatives a better bet. "I know of no reporting mechanism that would come close to describing and measuring the risks in a huge and complex portfolio of derivatives. Auditors can't audit these contracts, and regulators can't regulate them. When I read the pages of 'disclosure' in 10-Ks of companies that are entangled with these instruments, all I end up knowing is that I *don't* know what is going on in their portfolios (and then I reach for some aspirin)."[14]

Derivatives serve a purpose, but all too often they are used to devious ends, including a way to sneak around margin requirements and settlement periods. Investors should be hypersensitive to the excessive use of derivatives by corporations, hedge funds, big banks, and other large institutions.

"Derivatives are like sex," explained Buffett at one annual meeting. "It's not who we're sleeping with, it's who they're sleeping with that's the problem."

Margin—Investing with Borrowed Money

Using funds borrowed from your brokerage house, or margin, to leverage profits is tricky. While the Federal Reserve Bank limits margin debt to 50 percent of an investment, even that amount of margin can cause enormous trouble. The financial crisis of 2007–8 hinged largely on willy-nilly and unjustified credit practices, and not just in the housing industry.

"Margin debt owed on stocks listed on the New York Stock Exchange has surpassed $350 billion," wrote the Stock Broker Fraud Blog in July 2007. "This is up $35 billion, or over 10 percent, in just one month. The jump in margin debt brings new warnings to investors concerning the risks of leveraged investments."[15]

Ben Graham's warnings about using margin to leverage stock market profits were based on his own experiences. Graham had anticipated the crash of 1929, although he did not anticipate how overwhelming it would be and how long it would last. He had hedged many of his investments and took care to buy quality stocks, but he also was liberal in his use of margin. When the margin calls rolled in, one after another, his accounts were decimated. He and his partner Jerome Newman worked tirelessly and with no pay until their accounts were back in the black. It was a mistake they never made again. From that time on they avoided the use of margin. Other equally smart people have been snared by margin.

Bernie Ebbers, chairman of WorldCom and perpetrator of one of the largest acts of corporate fraud in U.S. history, was trapped by margin calls after the government intervened in some of WorldCom's business practices, and Ebbers's house of cards started folding. Ebbers's own enthusiasm for WorldCom drove him to load up on the company's common stock, which he typically purchased using his existing shares as collateral. When WorldCom's shares began to slide, Ebbers was suddenly faced with margin calls. He could have sold shares to meet the debt, but WorldCom's board of directors refused to authorize the sale of his insider shares because once the word was out that Ebbers was forced to sell, other shareholders would rush out the door behind him, driving the share price down even more.

Margin isn't necessarily a bad thing, but it must be used cautiously. The investor must be able to meet unexpected margin calls on stocks he has purchased, and he should be able to do so without being forced to sell other perfectly good stocks in his portfolio.

Points to Remember

"To be an outstanding long-term investor, it is totally necessary to actively seek superior results. It is very difficult to do that if you are an investor, have a job, family life, with no time or ability to do that type of analysis, or if you don't have behavioral characteristics to become an active investor," advised Charles Brandes. But, he added, "I'd rather be competitive, and I really think the active smart investor who has the basic fundamental knowledge or necessary behavior aspects still has an advantage."

When building a portfolio start with these concepts:

- Create an investment plan that is appropriate for your age, timeline, income level, and personality.

- Do your research and trust your own decisions.

- Realize that the most effective and the cheapest ways to hedge your positions are by avoiding credit, by diversification, and by building in a margin of safety.

- Don't panic when your stocks or the market is volatile. Do get worried if you believe your holdings or the market in general is getting crazy.

"We have new times and new products, but it gets back to the market there is to serve you and not to instruct you," Buffett reminds us.

As Irving Kahn once said, "Between the ultra-depression conservatism of Ben Graham and the brilliance of the monopoly investor Warren Buffett, there are ample levels that should fit your own pattern of risk to reward, suitable for your capital needs and lifestyle."[16]

Are You an Investor or a Gambler?

Many investors do not understand the nature of gambling or fail to recognize their tendency to gamble. Here are some of the signs of a person who believes she is investing but actually is gambling:

- Engages in speculative risk taking resulting in significant losses in relation to level of assets.

- Chases losses through increasing speculation or has difficulty stopping when losing.

- Borrows money in order to invest.

- Behavior appears erratic, inconsistent, or irrational, or trading is excessively frequent.

The Connecticut Council on Problem Gambling offers guidelines for responsible gambling. Almost all of these points apply equally to gambling and to out-of-control trading in the securities markets.

- Don't use money needed for daily living expenses.

- Set a dollar limit. Identify a specific amount of money you can afford to lose and stop when that amount of money is gone.

- Don't keep chasing losses and increase the risk of losing more money.

- Systematically set aside some of the winnings (profits) for other purposes.

For more information on the relationship between gambling and investing, and for help if you think you have a problem, go to the Connecticut Council on Problem Gambling Web site, www.ccpg.org.

Avoiding Fraudsters

Genuine value investors, those who learn about securities before they invest in them, are less susceptible to the type of financial fraud perpetrated by Bernie Madoff and those who misbehave like him. Ponzis and other types of fraudulent schemes seldom sway the stock market because the perpetrators were never invested in the market. The exception is fraud that takes place within corporate financial accounting, a subject that will be addressed later in this book. However, it is wise to watch for these red flags:

- Your financial adviser has custody of your assets. He can fully invest or sell and walk off with your money, as he pleases.

- Returns consistently are too good to be true. Check the typical returns for the field in which you are investing and question any returns that are too far outside the parameters of normal.

- You don't understand the investment, and your adviser tells you that it is too sophisticated for the average Joe to understand. That, the adviser explains, is what makes the investment so special.

- The investment is emotionally charged. There is pressure to act fast. The adviser flatters you with the idea that you are entering an exclusive club.

- The investment involves a euphoric community of investors, whether it be friends, family, or a religious organization. Church affiliations are especially dangerous, since that is the place where we most often abandon our fear to trust.

- The research or due diligence was done by someone else, and you're simply taking their word for it.

- An offer comes from a stranger over the Internet or on the telephone. The Internet is a brilliant tool for investors, but like other useful tools (chain saws, blowtorches), it can be misused. Scammers are turning to the Internet to modernize many old schemes, including the Ponzi and the practice of pumping and dumping stocks. The glossary at the back of this book contains definitions of these terms.

How to Avoid Investment Fraud

- Steer clear of products, schemes, or investment vehicles that you don't understand.

- Pass up high-risk stocks and bonds.

- Research the investment adviser and check with the Securities and Exchange Commission before investing. Especially investigate if it is an individual who seemingly works alone or with a very small group of people. Make sure the investment is what it seems to be. Is it licensed, registered, and properly listed? Do the organizers have prior records of investor fraud?

- Your gut tells you there's something wrong. Your gut is right more often than not, so listen to it.

What to Do About Financial Fraud

Report the incident to the appropriate government regulator for information and help.

The Securities and Exchange Commission has excellent advice and guidelines on scams and what to do about them. Check the Web site, www.sec.gov.

Chapter 6

The Balance Sheet

The field of investments has always been a
wonderful blend of science and art.[1]
DAVID IBEN, TRADEWINDS GLOBAL INVESTORS

We all have had the urge to scurry away from the flat, black-and-white pages of corporate financial statements, intimidated by rows of numbers, unsure of their relevance or reliability. But through the ages, sages have advised that to grow and make progress, we must face up to the things we fear the most. By taking the time to gain a rudimentary understanding of financial statements, you will find that the balance sheet and income statement are not as cold as they seem. In fact, they can become our friends. It is in these documents that we find, or at least confirm, intrinsic value.

There are three points to consider when studying financial statements:

- Assets tell about a company's stability, safety, and in many cases, its potential for growth.

- Debt diminishes assets and earnings, but also can be used to boost growth.

- The quality of earnings and potential earnings—of lack thereof—drives share prices either up or down.

Guidance on the first two points is found in the balance sheet, and the third is found in the income statement.

Clues to Safety

Graham told his students to face reality, to study the facts, and to forget about hunches, rumors, or personal feelings about what stocks and stock indexes may or may not do.

He said, "My reputation—such as it is, or perhaps as recently revived—seems to be associated chiefly with the concept of 'value.' But I have been truly interested solely in such aspects of value as present themselves in a clear and convincing manner derived from the basic elements of earning power and balance-sheet position, with no emphasis at all placed on such matters as small variations in the growth rate from quarter to quarter, or the inclusion or exclusion of minor items in calculating the so-called 'primary earnings.' Most significant here, I have resolutely turned my back on efforts to predict the future."[2]

Graham's admonitions are well taken, but observation of and conversations with such investors as Warren Buffett, Charlie Munger, Peter Lynch, and others have shown that with education and experience, an investor's instincts and intuition are honed. The seasoned investor can almost smell a good deal, although the veteran will also look at the facts and work through the numbers before making an investment decision. Almost all investors have some instinct for trouble, and if our intuition tells us that something may be wrong, we should pay attention to that nagging inner voice.

Finding Intrinsic Value

There is endless debate about whether to focus on balance sheet information with emphasis on assets or on the income statement with emphasis on earnings. Early students of Graham and Dodd, such as Irving Kahn and Walter Schloss, emphasize the balance sheet and have wracked up impressive investment records because of it.

Kahn, who served as Graham's teaching assistant at Columbia University, says, "We stress balance sheets and assets. We're old fashioned because our paramount aim is preservation of capital."[3] His son Thomas, who was a partner at Kahn Brothers, added: "Stocks rarely get priced at sharp discounts from intrinsic value without the market perceiving, correctly or incorrectly, that there are troubles in the company. Our job is to analyze whether those troubles are permanent or temporary."[4]

Warren Buffett for many years held a different point of view. While he was keenly aware of debt and other balance sheet information, Buffett often emphasized the income statement. Yes, he was looking for quality, but he was also on a quest for growth. In recent years he has shifted partially back to assets that can sustain and help a company in times of extreme inflation.

To achieve a complete, balanced, three-dimensional portrait of a company, we need both reports. Using them, we can apply a "twofold test of value," cross-checking between the current position of a company and the direction in which the operation is moving.

Think of the process this way. If a corporation were a ship, the balance sheet would be the hull and the income statement would be the sails. The hull keeps the business afloat while the sails—propelled by sales—move it forward. Using the financial statements we can simplify information, plucking from them the details we need and want. Are the sails full and fluttering or are they slack? Is the ship flying the skull and crossbones of a pirate?

Let's start with the balance sheet.

Balance Sheet Elements

The balance sheet contains four key indicators. They are:

- Assets

- Debt

- Cash holdings

- Equity position (including dividends)

The Nature of Assets

There are many types of assets, ranging from inventories to manufacturing plans to a list of credit card customers. Corporate assets fall into two categories—tangible or intangible.

Tangible, or hard assets, refer to both cash and fixed assets such as land, buildings, equipment, and office furniture.

Cash is cash and can be accepted at face value. Cash, or liquidity, gives a company the ability to weather hard times and take advantage of opportunities to expand internally by developing new products and markets or externally by acquiring other companies.

Fixed assets, on the other hand, can be tricky to evaluate. If they are paid for or have appreciated, they can give a company enormous strength. Walgreens, for example, has valuable drugstore real estate, much of which was purchased long ago. Walgreens is the largest drugstore chain in the United States and its territories, with nearly 7,500 locations. This real estate, much of it on key street intersections, gives the company its competitive advantage.

Yet corporate assets can also be a drag on the company's energy.

The type and quality of assets is important. Many assets, such as planes for airlines or automobile assembly lines, must be constantly upgraded at high costs. If real estate is unusable rusted factories, outdated, inefficient equipment; or inventories that must be sold at a deep discount, hard assets are questionable.

The second type of assets is called soft or intangible, because they are more elusive in nature, making them even more difficult to evaluate than tangibles. Intangibles include goodwill, patents and trademarks, licenses, capitalized advertising costs, and other nonphysical resources. While it may be difficult to pin a price on these types of assets, they also can be the most important qualities of a company. The universally known brand names of Google, Coca-Cola, and McDonald's give these companies a moat that provides them with a strong advantage over competitors. To make things better, some of the intangibles have been acquired at a very low cost. Google, for example, until recently never advertised and spent almost no money promoting its services. Its dominance in the search engine field grew by word of mouth, costing the company practically nothing. Google is a prime example of a company with both valuable tangible assets (cash and an army of low-cost processing centers) and intangibles (its brand name, its talented workforce, and the imaginative services it offers).

Determining Book Value

Book value is nothing more than assets minus liabilities, although the debate arises over what to include in assets and what must be considered a liability. To calculate book value, start with total assets, and then subtract intangible assets, liabilities, and any stock issues ahead of common stock. This is the price you might pay for a company if you were buying the whole thing, or at least, it is a good starting point to determine how

Measuring Progress

"The ideal standard for measuring your yearly progress would be the change in Berkshire's per-share intrinsic value. Alas, that value cannot be calculated with anything close to precision, so we instead use a crude proxy for it: per-share book value."[5]

—Warren Buffett

much you should pay for the company. To figure the book value per share, divide the results by the total number of shares outstanding.

For example, a company with $2 billion in assets and $1.6 billion in liabilities has a book value of $400 million. If it has 20 million shares of common stock outstanding, its per-share book value is $20. Graham felt that a value stock should sell for 1.2 times tangible book value and preferably for less; therefore he would not pay more than $24 for the stock. Such stocks are not easy to find in normal markets but they do show up when the markets are distressed.

Any time the number of shares outstanding becomes part of an equation, check in the corporate financial statements, including the footnotes, to confirm that all shares, including all stock options and possible convertible shares, are included. Unless shareholder's equity is treated as fully diluted by these outstanding obligations, the calculations are meaningless.

The Beauty of Book Value

Book value is a time-tested and honored measure of a company's strength and its value to investors.

There have been times when book value was dismissed as rooted in the past and not particularly relevant to a company's future prospects. Earning capacity carried more weight. There is credence to this philosophy, since assets sometimes can be difficult to price or knowingly carried at a price that no longer applies. But, like other conservative measures, book value always seems more interesting when times are hard. When growth is tough to come by, stability saves the day.

In recent years, shares typically have sold for around three times book value, and before the adjustment of 2007, the price-to-book ratio often was extremely high. In 2007 Amazon was selling at the breathtaking P/B of 64. Boeing also had what was considered a high P/B at 13. Apple and Microsoft both had a P/B ratio of 8.7. All of these stocks could be considered to be on the pricey side.

In mid-2009 a writer for *Barron's* declared that Berkshire Hathaway was a bargain with a P/B ratio of 1.2 compared with Berkshire's typical P/B of 1.6 to 1.8 per share. The company's A shares were then selling at $85,000, down from a 2007 peak of $149,000 per share. Berkshire's book value was estimated at $72,000 to $73,000 per share.[6] Certainly it was a stock Graham would be considering. In 2009 Berkshire's book value increased by 20 percent to $84,437 and its share price rose to $122,420, lowering its P/B to 1.4. *Barron's* clearly was correct in its analysis.

The Weakness of Book Value

Like all formulas and ratios used in the financial world, book value is not infallible. Book value serves as a better evaluation tool for industrial companies with a high proportion of fixed assets than it does for companies whose main assets are intellectual property, goodwill, and the softer kind. Shares of capital-intensive industries trade at lower price-to-book ratios because they generate lower earnings per dollar of assets. Business depending on human capital will often generate higher earnings per dollar of assets, so will trade at a higher price-to-book ratio. In most cases, investors can accept higher ratios for growth companies than for old-line, highly stable companies. However, it's usually easier to hang on to physical assets than it is to preserve intellectual or human capital.

Price-to-Book Ratio

One of the most familiar uses of book value involves comparing it with the stock's share price. The price-to-book ratio sets the floor for stock prices under a worst-case scenario. If a company is liquidated willingly or is forced into bankruptcy, the book value is what may remain for the owners after all the debts are paid. If a company's P/B is 1, that number suggests the investor will get all his investment back in liquidation, assuming assets can be resold at their book value. The higher the price-to-book ratio, the less likely there will be enough assets to pay all debts and have money left for shareholders.

The Debt Trap

If we've learned no other lesson in the first decade of the new millennium, it is to use borrowed money delicately and with a light touch. Just as it is with individuals and with nations, corporate debt is a liability and the interest paid for borrowed money is an expense.

Borrowed money can help a company meet obligations, smooth uneven cash flow, and accelerate growth. It is part of the capital structure of almost any business and allows management to develop new products, build new facilities, and expand into additional markets. But used carelessly, debt is a drag on assets and earnings and can pull the entire business down. The whole purpose of bankruptcy courts is to stave off creditors until a company can get back on its feet, or if recovery is not possible, to pay off debts in the most equitable way possible. Companies without debt may close their doors if business is bad, but they do not go into bankruptcy. For more on a company's ability to meet its debt obligation, read the section on EBITDA in the next chapter.

The Formerly Respected Bond Rating

Issuing bonds is one of the ways both governments and corporations borrow money. Corporate bond ratings have long been a measure for estimating how able the company is to repay its debts. Corporations that pose a default risk have lower ratings and therefore must accept a higher interest rate when borrowing. Those with a high rating can borrow more easily and pay a lower rate.

For decades the major bond rating agencies, such as Standard & Poor's, Moody's, and Fitch, were trusted organizations, and their debt analyses were held in the highest esteem. Investors in stocks could use the bond ratings issued by the major rating agencies as a significant sign of corporate stability.

"The credit rating agencies have played a pivotal role in the global debt markets for over thirty years," noted *MoneyWeek*, "with the stamp of approval from Moody's, Standard and Poor's or Fitch a prerequisite for the sale of a bond. The agencies' scale of ratings—from AAA for an issuer of unimpeachable creditworthiness, to the Cs and Ds for issuers of highly speculative or defaulted securities (often called 'junk')—form the basis of the capital markets."

Near the end of the last century, all that came into question. Prior to the 1970s, bond credit ratings agencies were compensated for their analysis by investors who wanted an impartial opinion on the creditworthiness of a corporation and of a particular offering. Then the three major ratings agencies began to be paid for their work by the securities issuers for whom they issued those ratings, which has led to the notion that the ratings are no longer objective. Additionally, the ratings companies became deeply involved in the issuance process itself, advising borrowers on how to get the desired ratings for new loans. Companies have been accused of shopping around for the best ratings from the three ratings agencies.

Following the 2001 Enron debacle, the financial media discovered that Moody's and S&P had maintained "investment grade" ratings on the company's debt until just four days before the Texas-based utility holding company filed for bankruptcy.[7]

Furthermore, it was trouble in the subprime credit markets that helped push the financial markets over the brink, and the ratings agencies got plenty of blame for that. "The US sub-prime market became the most egregious example of the abuse of the credit rating process and, ultimately, of common sense," explained *MoneyWeek*. "Mortgage loans made to lower-income and financially unsound Americans, who had in many cases lied about their incomes and borrowed many multiples of their (fictitious) salaries, were pooled and securitized, with their top-rated tranches granted the gold standard rating of AAA."[8]

By 2007 it was clear that lax bond rating was a terrible mistake. By then the overbuilt housing market began falling and many bond issues defaulted. "Eventually, when the AAA-rated tranches had lost up to 30 percent of their value, and the lower-rated pieces had become close to worthless, they moved to downgrade many of the issues," wrote *MoneyWeek*.[9]

Even though the 2010 financial reform legislation calls for stringent rules for rating agencies, there is little recourse except to return to the balance sheet to confirm that the debt information there aligns with the company's bond rating. Investors should ask two key questions, and the answers to both questions should be "yes":

- Are debt levels manageable?
- Once debts are paid, is there enough cash left to keep the business going and growing?

Debt-to-Equity Ratio

This formula shows the investor strength compared with debt, or how much equity is there to cushion creditors' claims in case the company faces liquidation.

$$\text{Debt-to-Equity Ratio} = \frac{\text{Total Liabilities}}{\text{Shareholder Equity}}$$

A healthy company maintains an approximated debt-to-equity ratio of 50 percent. This means that there is $1 of equity for every 50 cents of debt. When everything else is in good order, a company might be able to carry as much as 55 cents per $1 of equity, but never should debt go above this level.

Net Current Asset Value

Net current asset value, or working capital, is at the very heart of Ben Graham's investment principles.

An appropriate NCAV is a valuable financial cushion in any business cycle, allowing a company to finance its daily operation. A company's business cycle starts with the acquisition of raw materials, moves along to finished goods, and eventually ends in sales and money flowing into the bank account. When a company has sufficient working capital it can pay its current obligations from its current assets and weather all possible storms.

$$\text{Net Current Asset Value (working capital)} = \frac{\text{Current Assets (cash, accounts receivable, inventory)}}{\text{Current Liabilities}}$$

If possible, buy shares that are trading at two thirds the net current asset value per share. This gives a company a durable margin of safety.

Limits of NCAV as a Margin of Safety

Most companies trading below NCAV have small capitalization, under $100 million, and therefore fly below the radar of institutional investors. Because the market capitalization is limited, trading volume also may be low, making it difficult to accumulate enough shares to be meaningful. A determined investor may have to spread out purchases over a number of days to accumulate the number of shares he wants.

These NCAV stocks aren't easy to find, especially in a bull market atmosphere. Yet in 2008 there were, for a brief time, many to be found. Even when markets favor NCAV investors, the stocks must be studied to determine why they are so cheaply priced. When a company's market value is lower than its net current asset value, it may be considered more profitable to shut the company down and sell off its assets individually rather than continue to run it as a going concern. In that case the shareholders may share in the profits of the sale. Except for large predator investors, that's usually not what shareholders want. Instead, it would be preferable if management could turn things around so that shares become more attractive and the price rises.

For an added level of safety, Graham advised that a portfolio of low-NCAV stocks should:

- Contain a larger number of shares than the typical portfolio,

- Be extensively diversified to spread the risk, and

- Lean toward companies with acceptable earnings. Filter out companies with a pattern of unprofitability and without a concrete business strategy.

"Many NCAV stocks," writes Ravi Nagarajan for the Web site the Rational Walk, "have concentrated ownership profiles in which one individual or a small group controls the company. In such scenarios, it may be difficult or impossible to unlock the value in the company if the agenda of the controlling parties differs from our interests. For example, if the owners of a NCAV stock are also on the payroll, it is always possible for excessive compensation practices to divert the value from shareholders to the owners via payroll. Therefore examining whether the company has trustworthy management is important."[10]

Current Ratio

Another standard measure of working capital is the current ratio.

$$\text{Current Ratio} = \frac{\text{Current Assets}}{\text{Current Liabilities}}$$

As you can see, the current ratio has immediacy to it. It speaks to a company's present condition—what is happening at this moment. A current ratio of 2—meaning no more than $1 of current liabilities for

$2 of current assets—is ideal. A company should have debt of no more than 50 percent of its current assets. Companies with small inventories and easily collected receivables can carry a little more debt than a large company with less reliable cash flow.

Quick Ratio

The quick ratio is also called the acid test. It is a rigorous measure of a company's day-to-day muscle.

$$\text{Acid Test (Quick Ratio)} = \frac{\text{Current Assets} - \text{Inventory}}{\text{Current Liabilities}}$$

A quick ratio of 1 indicates that a company can meet its obligations in the event that all sales suddenly stopped. As outrageous as this possibility sounds, think of the plight of airlines following the 9/11 terrorist attacks. The carriers could not fly, but still had to meet salaries, maintain equipment, make loan payments, and hold in place for several days until air traffic resumed. It was six weeks before all U.S. airports were open and normal flight schedules became possible. Even then many people were reluctant to fly, further depressing airline revenues. This tragedy was extremely damaging to airlines. Because the unexpected can happen and sometimes does happen, it is comforting if a company passes both the current ratio and the acid test.

Net-Nets

Value investors love to shop at fire sales. One of Graham's favorite quests was to search for stocks whose current assets are one third greater than the sum of current *and* long-term liabilities. His students affectionately called this the "used cigar-butt" approach. The cigar butt may be battered and lying in the gutter, but it has a few good puffs left in it, and it is free. An investor looking for deep discounts would have been joyous in late 2007 and through much of 2008. There were cigar-butt prices, even in companies that weren't practically used up. These stocks were selling at bottom-fisher prices, but investors were frightened and it took a while before they got back in the buying mood.

The keys to success with this method are patience, when looking for equities to purchase, and accumulating a fairly large and well-diversified group of stocks. You may lose money on one third of the purchases, one third will malinger and not show much growth, but one third are likely to do so well that they make up for the laggards.

Net-Net Asset Value per Share

$$= \frac{\text{Current Assets} - \text{Current Liabilities} - \text{Long-term Debt}}{\text{Number of Shares Outstanding}}$$

The High Cost of Accounting Fraud

The years 2001 and 2002 were heartbreakers in regard to the unprecedented number of gaudy and egregious corporate scandals. The wayward companies included Enron, Tyco, Global Crossing, and the largest of all—the $11 billion WorldCom fraud.

WorldCom, which also came up under the subject of margin debt, was the United States' second largest long-distance phone company after AT&T. Under the leadership of the charismatic and well-liked Bernie Ebbers, WorldCom grew primarily by aggressively acquiring other telecommunications companies, most notably MCI Communications. Between 1991 and 1997 WorldCom spent nearly $60 billion in about sixty-five acquisitions and in the process accumulated

$41 billion in debt. Nevertheless, the company was a darling of Wall Street and analysts and brokers encouraged investors to load up on the stock.

All these acquisitions in such a short time were not easy to handle; service declined and there was confusion in the accounting department, a situation that lends itself conveniently to fraud.

WorldCom loosely interpreted generally accepted accounting principles (GAAP) when preparing financial statements. To make it look like profits were increasing, WorldCom wrote down in one quarter millions of dollars in newly acquired assets while simultaneously charging against earnings the cost of expected future expenses. This resulted in bigger losses in the current quarter but smaller ones in future quarters, making it appear that profits were steadily improving. It all worked out well as long as WorldCom continued making acquisitions, but when in 2002 the government would not allow WorldCom to buy Sprint, the scheme began to crumble. Additionally, an internal auditor at the company became suspicious of other accounting procedures intended to deceive investors. Heroically the auditor worked quietly on evenings and weekends and eventually went to the board of directors' audit committee with her findings. WorldCom filed for bankruptcy protection in the summer of 2002 and subsequently admitted to $9 billion of accounting deceit.

In the summer of 1999 WorldCom shares were trading at $64. By May 2002, the shares were worth mere pennies. Billions of dollars in market value had evaporated, and three years later Ebbers was sentenced to twenty-five years in prison. But WorldCom wasn't alone in its treachery and Ebbers wasn't the only one to go to jail. Executives from Dynegy Inc., Adelphia Communications, Tyco, and other corporations also were convicted of various types of accounting malfeasance.

Sarbanes–Oxley Cracks Down

As a reaction to this flurry of corporate fraud, the Sarbanes–Oxley Act (SOX) was enacted in mid-2002, introducing major changes to the regulation of financial practice and corporate governance. The legislation, which does not apply to privately held firms, established new or enhanced standards for all U.S. public company boards, management, and public accounting firms. It created a quasi-public agency, the Public Company Accounting Oversight Board, or PCAOB, in charge of overseeing, regulating, inspecting, and disciplining accounting firms in their roles as auditors of public companies. SOX also covers issues such as auditor independence, corporate governance, internal control assessment, and enhanced financial disclosure.

Sarbanes–Oxley has made listed companies much more transparent to shareholders. Management, under the keen eye of external auditors, now must ensure that adequate internal controls are in place and that financial numbers are accurate. The statute can impose stiff civil and criminal fines and penalties for noncompliance.

Nevertheless, critics claim that SOX is overly complex, that it costs corporations too much to comply, and it makes the United States less competitive internationally. Its supporters insist, however, that tough laws are necessary if we expect domestic and foreign investment money to flow into the U.S. stock markets.

The Basics

Graham and Dodd taught the importance of book value, equity, low debt-to-equity ratios, and other ways of testing the core strength of a corporation. While a share price near to the asset value of a company is not a guarantee of a generous total return in the future, it is a good place to begin.

Graham also explained that "stocks sell on earnings and dividends, and not on cash-asset values—unless distribution of the cash assets is in prospect."[11]

So now we look for earning power. We go in search of positive price-to-earnings ratios, low costs, desirable products, strong sales, and good future earnings prospects. These characteristics will be deviled out of the income statement.

Quick and Easy Formulas and Ratios

$$\text{Book Value} = \frac{\text{Total Assets} - \text{Intangible Assets} - \text{All Liabilities} - \text{Stock Issues}}{\text{Number of Common Shares Outstanding}}$$

$$\text{Debt-to-Equity Ratio} = \frac{\text{All Liabilities}}{\text{Total Shareholder Equity}}$$

$$\text{Net Current Asset Value} = \text{Current Assets} \div \text{Current Liabilities}$$

$$\text{Current Ratio} = \frac{\text{Current Assets}}{\text{Current Liabilities}}$$

$$\text{Net Quick Asset Value} = \text{Current Assets} - \text{Inventory} - \text{Current Liabilities}$$

$$\text{Quick Ratio} = \frac{\text{Current Assets} - \text{Inventory}}{\text{Current Liabilities}}$$

$$\text{Net-Net} = \text{Current Assets} - \text{Current Liabilities} - \text{Long-term Debt}$$

$$\text{Net-Net Asset Value per Share} = \frac{\text{Current Assets} - \text{Current Liabilities} - \text{Long-term Debt}}{\text{Number of Common Shares Outstanding}}$$

$$\text{Price/Earnings Ratio} = \frac{\text{Share Price}}{\text{Earnings per Share}}$$

$$\text{Profit Margin as a Percentage} = \frac{\text{Gross Profit} \times 100}{\text{Total Shares}}$$

$$\text{Free Cash Flow Yield} = \frac{\text{Free Cash Flow per Share}}{\text{Share Price}}$$

Discounted Cash Flow Model = Discounted Present Value

$$= \frac{\text{Future Value}}{(1 + \text{interest rate})^n} = \text{Future Value} \ (1 - \text{discount rate})^n$$

Chapter 7

The Only Growth Rate That Counts: Earnings[1]

Value investing is just standard economics.
Think logically about what you are doing. Think about it without
emotion. And think about what makes sense.[2]

ANDREW WEISS

When viewed in tandem with the balance sheet, the income statement helps the investor see what it is that makes a company grow. While the balance sheet is a static view of a company, a snapshot frozen at a certain time, the income statement represents the company's vitality. The earnings statement, often called the profit and loss statement, represents the corporation in motion. Put the balance sheet and profit and loss reports together with the statement of retained earnings and the statement of cash flow, and the operation becomes multidimensional. Both the structure and the fluidity of a business enterprise become visible.

A business that plugs away, year after year, producing a reliable income for its owners is a terrific asset. But unless the income increases over time, the value of the business does not grow. "That's the only growth rate that really counts: earnings," said Peter Lynch.[3]

The Secrets of the Income Statement

Bill Gates once noted that business wasn't all that hard to understand. You add up how much money you earned, add up all of your expenses, subtract the expenses from the earnings and you'll know if you are making a go of it. That's it in a nutshell, but in a big, complex corporation, the bookkeeping gets vastly more complicated.

A company should produce enough income to cover operating expenses, pay back debt, meet a dividend obligation if there is one, and still have money left over to shovel back into the business to fuel future earnings growth. Investors expect to share in the growth, either by receiving dividends or through increased share price. This is their incentive for taking money out of their safe savings accounts to buy ownership of a public company.

The income statement, as Gates implied, is divided into two sections: revenues and expenses. Revenues include sales figures for products or services, profits from the sale of any assets, such as real estate or a subsidiary company, rents, interest earned, and various other items that bring money into the company. Under the expenses category is found the cost of producing the goods or services, overhead expenses, depreciation, research and development costs, taxes, and other business costs.

Honest Income

All too often, when management fiddles with the books, it is the profit and loss statement that is jiggered; accounting can be a highly creative activity. Graham noted that the income statement was fertile ground for what he satirized as the "experimental accounting laboratory." Always read the footnotes in a financial statement in case there is monkey business in the treatment of such items as nonrecurring profits or losses, operations of subsidiaries, depreciation of assets, and anything that is deferred.

Income often looks strong due to the one-time sale of an asset, such as real estate or a product line. This isn't necessarily a distortion, but it is never beneficial if the company is using a windfall to cover ordinary expenses. A one-time event helps the investor only if the money is used to:

- Restore the asset base, such as upgrading a manufacturing facility,

- Reduce debt and therefore reduce the cost of doing business, or

- In some way contribute substantially to future earnings.

Fortunately, manipulation of the income statement tends to distort earnings only in a single year, or over a relatively short time period. Eventually the ruse shows up.

Honest Adjustments

Sometimes items are "written down" or "written off" corporate books entirely, and this may be a legitimate business tactic. These adjustments can help investors in several ways. For example, if it becomes clear that a debt will never be collected or an asset—such as an old piece of equipment made obsolete by a new one—is no longer worth what it once was, the rewriting of its value helps investors see a more realistic picture of the company.

At times, investors overreact to a one-time blow to income and the share price of the company falls. A canny investor can take advantage of the anxiety attack to buy shares at a low price.

Be aware, however, that corporate management sometimes saves these write-downs for periods when earnings were not so good anyway. Better to pile all the bad news into one reporting period than to have it take the glory away from a good quarter. In the fiscal period following the write-off, earnings may appear to jump. This spike in earnings excites some investors, who see it as a trend rather than a reversion to the norm. Mistakes such as this can be avoided by looking at the numbers over a period of time and by reading the financial statements.

When studying earnings trends, be sure to compare like quarter to like quarter, for example, the spring quarter of 2009 to the spring quarter of 2010. Some companies have high sales prior to or during the Christmas season and lower sales in the spring. High and low seasons vary from business to business. Some retailers, for example, only stay in business so they can reap profits during the winter holiday season. And some profit from the beginning of the school year, while others depend on summer tourism for their strongest season.

A Perspective on Earnings

To smooth out short-term distortions, chart income statement figures over a span of seven to ten years. Buffett claims he sometimes looks at these figures over many decades. In this way both trends and aberrations become visible. Average out the numbers to get more typical sales, income, or expense figures. The longer the averaging process, the more you can rely on it as a measure of typical performance. Graham stressed the importance of a long view. "Stability," he said, "is assessed by the trend of per-share earnings over a ten-year period, compared with the average of the most recent three years. No decline represents 100 percent stability."[4]

He also coached his students to look at the nature, the quality, and the predictability of earnings.

An income statement is best viewed from three perspectives:

- Accounting—Are the earnings valid? Do they accurately reflect the condition of the business?

- Business—While the past does not always predict the future, it can give clues. Does the income statement show a dynamic, going, growing concern?

- Investment—What does this information mean in terms of share price?

Indicators of Growth

Graham considered a company to be on a progressive path when:

- Earnings have doubled in the most recent ten years, and

- They have declined by no more than 5 percent twice in the past decade.

These two conditions represent stability, although stability on its own is not enough. As was the case with assets, we also search for solid confirmation that growth is coming.

Peter Lynch pointed out that "there are five basic ways a company can increase earnings: reduce costs; raise prices; expand into markets; sell more of its products to the old markets; or revitalize, close or otherwise dispose of losing operations."[5]

Sales

The value investor's goal is to find companies with solid financial footing whose sales and earnings are growing faster than both their competitors and the economy in general. Generally speaking, share prices increase in value at about the same rate that sales grow. For dominant corporations in major industries, sales should grow at a rate of 5 percent to 7 percent per year. Growth companies' sales should increase at an even faster rate. Within the overall portfolio, the companies should have an average sales growth rate of about 10 percent. Not every company will achieve its sales goals each year. Some industries, such as housing, are cyclical; a company's production facility may be hit by a hurricane; other companies may enjoy increased sales because they are supplying much-needed goods and services to disaster victims. There may be surges and setbacks, but the average growth of sales over time should climb ever higher.

Income Gets Us to Profits

A company may have a great product that sells well and brings in income. But that isn't enough. For investors, there is more to it. Costs must be controlled. The company must have a strong profit margin and free cash flow, provide a return on equity, and have other qualities.

There are many measures of profitability. Graham's favorite indication of strength or weakness was the ratio of operating income to sales. The rating agencies may report the operating income as a percentage of revenue, or more commonly, the profit margin.

$$\text{Profit Margin} = \frac{\text{Gross Profits}}{\text{Net Sales}}$$

The formula produces a ratio. To express profit margin as a percentage, multiply the result by 100.

Profit margin is an indicator of a company's pricing policies, cost control, efficiency, and competitiveness.

Profit margins can vary drastically from business to business and from industry to industry. Discount airlines, for example, have a profit margin of around 11 percent. The software industry has a profit margin of 27 percent.

When the net profit margin of a company is low compared with its competitors, the share price suffers, and when it improves, the price is likely to rise. The best investment sometimes is a company with a low profit margin compared with others in its industry, but with a strong likelihood that a turnaround is in the works. Corporate restructuring or new management is often the catalyst for improved profit margins.

EBIT and EBITDA

Another accounting measure of profitability is earnings before interest and taxes (EBIT). Also known as operating income, EBIT is a measure of a firm's profitability, excluding interest and income tax expenses.

$$\text{EBIT} = \text{Operating Revenue} - \text{Operating Expenses (OPEX)} + \text{Nonoperating Income}$$

EBIT's next of kin, EBITDA, is earnings before interest and taxes and before depreciation and amortization.

EBITDA first came to investors' attention with leveraged buyouts in the 1980s, when it was used to indicate a company's ability to pay interest on outstanding debt. In time it became popular in industries with expensive assets that had to be written down over long periods of time.

"EBITDA is now commonly quoted by many companies, especially in the tech sector—even when it isn't warranted," reports Investopedia. "A common misconception is that EBITDA represents cash earnings. EBITDA is a good metric to evaluate profitability, but not cash flow."

As with other metrics such as beta, EBITDA is only useful if used properly and in conjunction with other measures of performance. One significant weakness is that it leaves out the cash needed to fund working capital and the replacement of outdated equipment. Unfortunately, EBITDA is sometimes used as a ruse to make a company's earnings look better than they are.

Retained Earnings

When all the income is counted, all the debts are settled, and dividends have been paid to shareholders, there may be money remaining. The undistributed profits or retained earnings become an asset and show up on the balance sheet rather than the income statement. As cash that can be used to grow the company, retained earnings are central to share price appreciation.

While these stores of cash are an asset, they can also put a company at risk. Corporate raiders are attracted to retained earnings as surely as bears go after spawning salmon. When management retains earnings with no apparent or pending use for the cash cache, the company often becomes a takeover target. Despite the comfort and advantages of cash reserves, they tend to make investors nervous. Investors often go by the motto, "use it or lose it."

More information is found on the company's statement of retained earnings, which explains any changes to retained earnings over the reporting period. If the retained earnings have increased it's informative to learn what produced the abundant earnings. Was it a windfall unlikely to happen again, or does it represent a trend? If the retained earnings drop, it is essential to find out why. If the cash was used to build the company's strength in some way, that is good. It is a red flag if earnings were used to make up for some shortfall or for some other purpose that doesn't promote the company's general well-being or progress.

Free Cash Flow

"One of the principles of finance focuses on the importance of cash because it is the life blood of a business and the primary means of creating shareholder value," writes Arthur Q. Johnson in his Mundoval Fund newsletter. "Free cash flow, or what Warren Buffett prefers to call 'owners earnings,' is the cash generated from the business in excess of the capital expenditures required to maintain the existing cash flow stream of the business."[6]

Free cash flow yield indicates the overall cash per share that a company is expected to earn against its stock price.

$$\text{Free Cash Flow Yield} = \frac{\text{Free Cash Flow per Share}}{\text{Share Price}}$$

This metric is similar to earnings yield, which is usually meant to measure generally accepted accounting principles (GAAP) earnings per share divided by share price. Generally, the lower the ratio, the less attractive the investment is and vice versa. The logic behind this is that investors prefer to pay as little per share as possible for as much earnings as possible.

Some investors regard free cash flow (which takes into account capital expenditures and other ongoing costs a business incurs to keep itself running) as a more accurate representation of the returns shareholders receive from owning a business, and thus prefer using free cash flow yield over earnings yield as an indicator of vitality.

The Power of Cash on Hand

Although Warren Buffett warns of the danger of holding too much cash in inflationary times, Berkshire Hathaway is a perfect example of how having strong cash reserves allows a company to survive and even prosper during times of crisis. In Berkshire's 2009 annual report, Buffett told the following story:

"When the financial system went into cardiac arrest in September 2008, Berkshire was a supplier of liquidity and capital to the system, not a supplicant. At the very peak of the crisis, we poured $15.5 billion into a business world that could otherwise look only to the federal government for help. Of that $9 billion went to bolster capital at three highly regarded and previously secure American businesses that need—without delay—our tangible vote of confidence. The remaining $6.5 billion satisfied our commitment to help fund the purchase of Wrigley, a deal that was completed without pause, while, elsewhere, panic reigned."[7]

Discounted Cash Flow Model

Discounted cash flow (DCF) is another valuation method based on income statement information and used to estimate the value of an investment. DCF analysis is a fairly complex formula that uses future free cash flow projections and discounts them (frequently using the weighted average cost of capital) to arrive at a present value of a security. There are many variations when it comes to what is used for cash flows and the discount rate in DCF analysis.

If the DCF value is higher than the current cost of the investment, the company is selling at a discount to future earnings and the opportunity looks attractive. Luckily it's not always necessary to do this calculation yourself. The information may be available in various share price analyses readily available on the Internet or at the reference desk of your local library.

The purpose of DCF analysis is to estimate the money you would receive from an investment and to adjust that amount for the time value of money. Put another way, DCF helps evaluate the investment considering the erosion of inflation and if the investment had simply earned a fixed interest rate over a period of time. In addition to investment finance, the discounted cash flow model is widely used in real estate development and corporate financial management.

Discounted cash flow models are powerful, but they have weaknesses. Since DCF is merely a mechanical valuation tool, the model is subject to the saying, "garbage in, garbage out." Small changes in inputs can result in large and often misleading changes in the perceived value of a company.

The Price-to-Earnings Ratio

In much of his later life, Graham strove to perfect a formula for intrinsic value. He never found an accurate and reliable formula. The best that investors can do is look at the handful of essential formulas and ratios described in this book (see chapter 6). One of the most useful is the price-to-earnings ratio. The P/E ratio is yet another indicator of the company's earning power. A high P/E ratio shows that investors expect earnings growth to be robust; a low P/E indicates gloomy expectations.

When per-share earnings for the past four quarters are divided into the share price, the result is the P/E ratio. A company with earnings of $3 per share with shares trading at $30 has a P/E of 10. In other words, the shares are selling at 10 times earnings. A trailing P/E is calculated using last year's earnings. The leading P/E is purely speculative because it relies on estimated future earnings.

As William O'Neil points out, the P/E ratio is not the cause of a stock going up. "It is the end result of a superior product and accelerating sales." In other words, the ratio is a distillation of the qualities that make a company work well.

Like other investment formulas, the P/E ratio should be used with caution. Earnings, after all, are ever moving and can be unpredictable. The ratio has little meaning except in comparison with the company's previous performance and the P/E ratios of other companies in the same industry. Graham used the following guidelines:

- He liked to buy stocks with a multiple of no more than 7 to 20 times earnings.

- He completely shunned stocks with a P/E above 20 times the previous year's earnings or 25 times the average earnings of the previous seven years.

Graham's ability to purchase stocks at those low multiples showed his willingness to dig deep, and to a large extent, it also reflected the times in which he was working. Investors today, including Buffett and William O'Neil, often are willing to buy stocks with a P/E well above 20, even 50 or higher, because they've discovered that exceptional companies with the best growth potential tend to have higher P/Es.

The Parameters of Share Price

Think of assets and earnings as two bookends at each end of a desirable share price. Assets, as indicated by book value, are a minimum price at which the security should sell, while the P/E establishes the upper range of price.

Therefore, if you determine that the appropriate book value for a company is $10 per share, any price below that should be questioned. If the company is in a cyclical industry—such as manufacturers of automobiles or kitchen appliances—the share price may simply reflect a cyclical low in the business. If the stock is selling for a cigar-butt price simply because of short-term or perceived problems, it may be a great buy. On the other hand, if the company is selling poorly because its technology is outdated, its research and development is faltering, or its commodity, such as coal or oil, is near depletion, pass on it.

If it seems to you that the appropriate P/E ratio for a stock is 10, the share price paid should be no more than 10 times the most recent year's earnings per share. Like most of our rules, this one also has an exception. Promising growth and high-technology companies frequently trade at P/Es of 30, 40, 50, or more. Since Graham would not touch stocks selling at those levels he would never buy IBM, although he was impressed with IBM products and the company share price skyrocketed in the early years.

There are many times when Buffett and other value investors break away from this limiting aspect of Graham's philosophy. When diversifying holdings it often makes sense to include high-tech or biotech stocks in the mix, and the best of these companies are likely to have high P/E ratios. The same is true of companies with hot new technologies.

O'Neil points out that Genentech (a pioneer in genetic engineering technology) and Syntex (which first brought out the birth control pill) had huge share price growth even after P/Es were in the hundreds. Both companies had explosive new products that sold very well. "We take the position, don't argue with the P/E if everything else is right."

Growth Stocks

Companies with a fast growth rate provide important vitality to a stock portfolio. But along with high growth comes heightened risk. Nothing proves that more than the collapse of high-tech markets at the end of the twentieth century. Sad news notwithstanding, glad is the investor who can use value principles to find a great growth stock. We will explore that concept more in chapter 9.

Points to remember:

- The companies most attractive to investors are those with consistent profitability.

- Look for a steady upward trend in earnings.

- Look for a P/E that is low compared with others in the same industry.

- When making estimates, be conservative. The underestimation provides a margin of safety.

Google Inc.

Google is one of the great business stories of the early twenty-first century, not only because of the founders' amazing understanding of the power of the Internet, but because of their remarkable business strategy. With no real business experience, Larry Page and Sergey Brin created an Internet company with genuine promise for long-term survival. With strong sales growth, gross margins, cash reserves, and no debt, Google was uniquely positioned to survive a severe economic downturn.

Two young Stanford University graduate students launched the Internet company in 1998. Even though Silicon Valley was in a slump at the time, Google went public in 2004 at $85 per share, raising $1.67 billion in capital. The original public offering had several striking features, including the fact that the company already had a history of sales. This is uncommon among Silicon Valley start-ups. By mid-2007 Google's shares were trading just under $720 per share.

Google is the world's dominant search engine provider, maintaining a massive index of Web sites and other online content. Google makes this information freely and instantly available to anyone with an Internet connection virtually anywhere in the world. Page and Brin redefined the word "media" with their automated search technology. The company generates revenue primarily by delivering laser-targeted online advertising linked to the subject of a search. Businesses like using Google's AdWords program to promote their products and services because they have enormous control over the message and can collect a great deal of information on those who are reading their ads.

Despite its popularity and inherent strength, Google's share price was seriously affected by the stock market crash of 2007–8.

But a look at the corporate fundamentals will show why the company's business model and practices sustained it. Google had cash reserves of $86 billion and carried no debt. It has had a five-year average growth rate of 71.6 percent with 2008 sales of $227 billion. The net profit margin was 22 percent. After a fifty-two-week low of $264, by mid-2010 Google's shares approached the $474, even though in the second quarter of that year both revenue and net income rose 24 percent.

Chapter 8

The Measure
of Management

Integrity without knowledge is weak and useless, and knowledge without integrity is dangerous and dreadful.

Samuel Johnson (1709–1784)

The financial roller coaster the world economy experienced between 2000 and 2009 confirmed something that most people already knew: honest, sound, responsible corporate management is essential to sustaining a healthy economy and a well-functioning stock market. Driven in various instances by greed, excessive competitiveness, incompetence, risk taking, or the sense that they needed to be doing what other companies were doing, corporate management made some dreadful early-century choices. Without a doubt government deregulation went too far, undoubtedly there was lax enforcement of the laws in place, but that is no excuse for flawed and failed management.

How do we determine if the companies we are evaluating are well managed? There are many yardsticks. Warren Buffett and his partner Charlie Munger measure themselves by Berkshire Hathaway's financial results when compared with the S&P 500. "Selecting the S&P 500 as our bogey was an easy choice," writes Buffett, "because our shareholders, at virtually no cost, can match its performance by holding an index fund. Why should they pay us for merely duplicating that result?"[1]

There are other measuring sticks as well, and each of them feeds right into the bottom line.

Integrity Is Essential

The woeful tales of Enron and WorldCom give us an idea of what can happen when leaders ignore both the law and their responsibility to shareholders. Buffett often says that he looks for "wonderful castles (good businesses), surrounded by deep, dangerous moats (barriers to entry), where the leader inside is an honest and decent person."[2]

Because the law is nothing more than the very least required behavior, the finest corporate leaders realize that they must operate within the law and then do even better.

Assurant, the huge insurance company, has a twenty-five-page corporate code of ethics that puts forth the notion that good behavior is in the best interest of shareholders. "We are committed to providing long-term value to our shareholders," states Assurant's code of ethics. "This will be accomplished by observing the highest standards of business practices and ethical conduct in all of our business dealings."

Investor's Business Daily founder William O'Neil points out that when corporations do not operate honestly and fairly, the situation tends to correct itself rather quickly. These companies eventually get their "just deserts," says O'Neil. "Bear markets clean up a lot of that."

Just because you can do something doesn't mean you should do it. Within the capitalist system, this is the place where judgment and integrity intersect with opportunity.

Wrong Turn into Yesterday[3]

Companies that stumbled early in the recent financial crisis were those directly involved in overbuilt and overlent home construction and mortgage lending, such as Britain's Northern Rock and the U.S. lender Countrywide Financial, as their credit sources dried up. More than one hundred mortgage lenders went bankrupt during 2007 and 2008. Concerns that investment bank Bear Stearns would collapse in March 2008 resulted in its hasty sale to JPMorgan Chase. The crisis peaked in September and October 2008 when several major institutions either failed, were acquired under duress, or were taken over by the government. These included once highly respected institutions such as Lehman Brothers, Merrill Lynch, Fannie Mae, Freddie Mac, and the global insurer AIG. Thirty-seven companies were dropped from the S&P 500 during that time because they went broke or no longer met the standards for inclusion.

The Stakeholders

Graham and Dodd, in *Security Analysis*, declared that "corporations are in law the mere creatures and property of the shareholders who own them; the officers are only the paid employees of the stockholders; the directors, however chosen, are virtually trustees, whose legal duty is to act solely in behalf of the owners of the business."[4]

On the face of it, this makes it seem that corporations are nothing more than entities of law that are accountable only to their legal owners, the shareholders. And yet even Graham and Dodd knew that unless corporations met their broader obligations to society they would not long exist.

According to contemporary thought, public corporations must balance the interests of their owners and those who manage them; creditors who loan them goods, services, or money; the employees who contribute their labor; the clients they serve; and not least, shareholders who invest their financial capital. All of these elements work together to produce value and generate corporate income. Together they are the oars that keep the business and the economy moving forward.

Who Manages?

John Bogle especially insists that U.S. corporations suffer from a situation in which professional management is separated from ownership, and there is no particular loyalty to a company, product, employees, or corporate mission.

He blames much of the early twenty-first century trouble in the financial markets on the concept that companies are being controlled by nonowners who have no dog in the fight. Too little of their own money is invested in the companies they run.

Additionally, too often the boards of directors are not truly independent, but rather closely linked with and in some way beholden to the person who appoints them, the CEO.

As the highest governing authority within the management structure of publicly traded companies, it is the board's job to choose and evaluate the CEO and to approve executive compensation. The board also must recommend and approve dividend payments, stock splits, and share repurchase programs, review and approve financial statements, and weigh in on acquisitions and mergers.

The SEC has issued specific guidelines on what constitutes an independent board member, and how many independents a board must have. Unfortunately, even these guidelines have not prevented CEOs from packing the board with people who will go along with their policies, pay packages, and perks.

The Independent Corporate Directors Association (ICDA) describes the SEC guidelines as the minimum required by the law, and stresses that good corporate governance often calls for stricter measures. Overall the ICDA encourages a code of ethics by which the board:

- Promotes and protects shareholder participation and long-term interests,

- Represents all shareholders of the company, not just those who may have nominated or elected them, and

- Stays focused on fiduciary duties, not subordinated to the promotion of any social, economic, environmental, or political program, however worthy.[5]

A shareholder's best defense against mismanagement is to seek out organizations in which the leadership has a deep financial stake in the company's future. We've often mentioned two such companies in this book—Berkshire Hathaway and Google Inc. Critics claim that decisions are too much in the hands of ownership in these companies. In both cases the shares are set up so that owners control the company, in both cases the company has been noted (and sometimes criticized) for holding large amounts of cash, and in both cases the company has profited in and from a poor economic climate.

Managing Like an Owner

Charles Brandes always prefers companies in which management has a meaningful ownership position. "If a president owns 20 percent or more of the shares outstanding, then we both want the same thing—increased share price. Managers tied only by salary and benefits aren't rowing the same boat as shareholders."[6]

Buffett also is on the alert for companies in which management has a large ownership position, or a strong family has such a dominant ownership position that they can remove unethical or underperforming top executives. This is the case at Berkshire itself, where Buffett and Munger often say "we eat our own cooking."[7] Both men have a large majority of their families' wealth tied up in Berkshire Hathaway.

What Good Managers Cannot Do

Benjamin Graham and Warren Buffett shared common core beliefs, but they differed in some important ways. Graham, a rather introverted, unsociable man, saw no benefit in visiting a company or meeting with management. The balance sheet and income statement, he felt, spoke for themselves. Buffett, although he doesn't spend a lot of time on company visits, regularly sings the praises of talented managers. Literally—he sometimes sings about them at the annual meeting, accompanying himself on a ukulele. Both Graham and Buffett, however, agree on a major point. A fundamentally poor business will remain a poor business, no matter how great the management. A talented jockey may make the most of a good racehorse, but he cannot make a poky pony run significantly faster. And, as Graham pointed out, in the end, the truth will always come out in the numbers.

Never Too Much Information

Despite Graham's reluctance to get cozy with management, events of the past thirty years or so have shown that investors need to be aware of everything that is going on and use that compilation of information to sharpen their investment skills.

"The laws and rules that govern the securities industry in the United States derive from a simple and straightforward concept: all investors, whether large institutions or private individuals, should have access to certain basic facts about an investment prior to buying it, and so long as they hold it," writes the Securities and Exchange Commission in its "What We Do" manifesto. "To achieve this, the SEC requires public companies to disclose meaningful financial and other information to the public. This provides a common pool of knowledge for all investors to use to judge for themselves whether to buy, sell, or hold a particular security. Only through the steady flow of timely, comprehensive, and accurate information can people make sound investment decisions."[8]

Thanks to the Internet, the vast amount of information held by the SEC regarding publicly traded companies is available rapidly and easily to anyone. The fact that few people actually use the information available to them gives the serious investor an advantage.

Management Vision

When Ted Turner launched CNN in 1980, when Bill Gates quit Harvard in 1975 to start Microsoft, when in 1998 Larry Page and Sergey Brin misspelled a nerdy word (googol—1 followed by 100 zeros) and created Google, they each had something in common. They had the single most important element that management brings to the corporate party: vision. Instantly and instinctively, each recognized a technology that would advance the path of civilization in some way. They saw an opportunity to create a business based upon something the world would need and want, even though the world didn't yet know it needed or wanted that product. Once these business innovators knew where they were going, they persevered until they were able to execute their plans.

Few corporate leaders can live up to the example set by Steve Jobs, cofounder of Apple, NeXT, and Pixar. Jobs and his partner Steve Wozniak launched the first successful personal computer manufacturing company in the 1970s. They and Apple went through several dramatic cycles, and as a result Jobs left the company in 1985. Apple went into steady decline until Jobs again took over in 1996, reenergizing the company that went on to develop the iPod, iPhone, and other popular electronic devices. Jobs is sometimes admired and sometimes criticized for his management style and Merlin-like skills of persuasion and salesmanship, but his vision trumps all.

"Here is something fascinating," says William O'Neil. "There were twenty-seven cycles showing the growth of America from the industrial age up until now. Every single new cycle is led by innovators, entrepreneurs and new inventions. In the 1870s it was railroads. They were an enormous benefit to society. Before railroads it took months and months to get [from the East] to the West Coast, if you made it at all. Then came the automobile and after that the airplane was invented. We've had radio, television, and the Internet. So it never ends. What we're seeing is that America is a country of innovators and inventors, always coming up with something newer, faster, better, cheaper. Management may not be ethical or so smart, government fouls up, but the system works very well. It keeps adjusting."

Charles Brandes says we must pay attention to "the rate of change in fundamentals for businesses, especially in the technology area. Things are changing more rapidly now than they did in the past. Take the film industry—Kodak, Fuji, and along came digital [photography]. We were always looking at that but thought film was still better than digital. Digital would become good enough to stand side by side with film, but film would be around for quite some time. That analysis was wrong and it hurt Kodak, which was a blue chip, nifty-fifty company for many years. That company now is really, really struggling. It is speculative right now. Because of rapid changes in technology, this is what happened to a really wonderful industry."

Shareholder Rights

The investment world has traveled down the path of trouble again and again. Prior to the great crash of 1929, there was an aversion to federal regulation of the securities markets, based on the belief that left to its own means, the economy would naturally follow the right course. This belief was particularly popular following World War I, when public interest in the stock market surged.

Excited by the concept of ownership, tempted by the promise of getting rich quick and the allure of easy credit, most investors of that era gave little thought to the risk inherent in the widespread abuse of margin financing and unreliable information about the companies in which they were investing. During the 1920s, approximately 20 million large and small investors got caught up in postwar prosperity and expected to make their fortunes in the stock market. Then came Black Friday and the stock market crash of 1929, followed by the Great Depression.

Suggestions that the federal government require financial disclosure and prevent the fraudulent sale of stocks were never seriously considered until it was too late. It is estimated that of the $50 billion in new securities offered during the 1920s, half became worthless.

When laws were finally enacted they had two main purposes:

- Companies publicly offering securities to investors must tell the public the truth about their businesses, the securities they are selling, and the risks involved in investing.

- People who sell and trade securities—brokers, dealers, and exchanges—must treat investors fairly and honestly, putting investors' interests first.

Although laws vary from state to state and country to country, shareholders in publicly held companies generally are considered to have certain main rights:

- Voting power on major issues including the election of directors and proposals for fundamental changes affecting the company such as mergers or liquidation. Voting takes place at the shareholder meeting or by proxy for those who cannot attend.

- Ownership in a portion of the company. In the event of a corporate liquidation, investors divide up the liquidated assets, although bondholders and preferred shareholders are paid before common stockholders. In a thriving business the ownership benefits accrue from the wise use of earnings and subsequent increase in share price.

- Right to sell their shares on a stock exchange. This privilege gives investors the ability to quickly return to cash if they choose to do so. Liquidity is one of the factors that differentiate stocks from investments such as real estate, collectibles, and so forth that usually take more time to sell.

- Common stock shareholders are entitled to common stock dividends if and when they are declared. Not all companies pay dividends, and some only pay them occasionally. Profits often are plowed back into the operation with the intention of making the company more profitable and therefore more valuable to shareholders.

- The right to see the company's financial statements and records. This opportunity is provided through public filings, including quarterly, annual, and other reports. Most of these reports are available through the SEC's EDGAR online service.

■ Shareholders may sue the company and its leaders for wrongful acts. Often this takes the form of a shareholder class-action lawsuit. After it was learned that WorldCom had grossly overstated 2002 earnings, giving shareholders and investors a false picture of its financial health, the telecom giant faced a rash of shareholder class-action suits. This right is now endangered by the possibility of tort reform, which leaves corporations with the right to sue but limits the rights of individuals. Some people advocate for limits on class-action lawsuits, a change that would give legal protection to deceitful management.

Sadly, having more and stiffer laws has not always prevented dishonest people from engaging in fraudulent practices. Furthermore, in the 1980s and later, the trend toward government deregulation removed some of the safeguards put in place following the Great Depression. The repeal of the Glass-Steagall Act, which created a barrier between commercial banking and investment banking, was particularly devastating. Business organizations pushed for the repeal on the grounds that it would be good for the economy. The business community routinely objects to regulations because of the costs and because of the fear of unintended consequences. In the end, however, financial disaster damages businesses as much as it does the rest of society. Having fair but tough laws gives shareholders some measure of protection.

Shareholder Responsibilities

Just as corporations and government regulators have rights and responsibilities, shareholders have rights and also have responsibilities. John Bogle says that in recent years professional money managers have not been vigilant stewards of the money entrusted to them. "In short," writes Bogle, "far too many of our corporate and financial agents have failed to honor the interests of their principals—the mutual fund investors and pension beneficiaries to whom they owed a fiduciary duty. The ramifications were widespread—for the failure of money managers to observe the principles of fiduciary duty played a major role in allowing our corporate managers to place their own interests ahead of the interests of their shareholders."[9]

Bogle calls upon both institutional investors, who should be defending their clients, and individual investors to be more responsible. As a shareholder, it is your job to:

- know with whom you are investing

- be informed about the securities you buy

- understand the investor's role in the overall economy

- if necessary, become an activist shareholder

"When I read the causes of the recent unpleasantness," concluded Bogle, "I haven't seen one single person who has said that the owners of these corporations, including the banking corporations, didn't seem to give a damn about how they were being run. We own all this stock but we pretty much do nothing."[10]

Despite all the attempts to get shareholders to cast their proxy votes, many do not because individual shareholders feel helpless in the face of company management, institutional investment managers, and other large shareholder groups. Nevertheless, there are many instances in which activist shareholders have effected change.

Evelyn Y. Davis is one of the best-known activist shareholders in the United States. She often is described as a "gadfly" shareholder by those who would characterize her as a frivolous troublemaker.

Davis, publisher of the *Highlights and Lowlights* newsletter for investors, is a shareholder in some eighty corporations. She has been attending shareholder meetings all over the United States since 1960.

To be sure, Davis is pushy and strident, often grilling management by asking difficult or embarrassing questions. However, she is a serious student of financial statements and SEC documents and often she is correct in her assessments and complaints. For example, in 2007 she introduced a shareholder's proposal to Goldman Sachs Group Inc. banning stock options as a management compensation tool. The options, she insists, encourage management to manipulate earnings in such a way as to receive options at an artificially low price and exercise them at an artificially high price. She also contended that the stock option grants "have gone out of hand in recent years and some analysts might inflate earnings estimates because earnings affect stock prices and stock options." She contended that there were better ways to compensate executives, including simply giving them stock rather than options.

While Davis was not backed up by institutional and other large holders of Goldman Sachs shares and her proposal failed, she received substantial coverage by Reuters news service, *The New York Times*, and other news outlets. She succeeded in starting a discussion about her concerns.

Granted, some activist shareholders are promoting personal or social causes that may not deserve the attention of other shareholders, but many times dissident shareholders make perfect sense and can serve as an early warning system for abuses.

Attend Some Annual Meetings: Become a Gadfly Shareholder

There are numerous reasons shareholders might want to attend annual meetings of the companies they own—at least some of the companies.

There is no better way to judge the quality of corporate management than by going to see and hear them in person and in action. You'll learn a lot. Are those running the company down to earth or are they pretentious? Nervous or calm? Are they open or do they evade questions?

If you had attended General Electric's meeting when Jack Welch was head of the company, you would have seen a brash, energetic, restless leader who constantly pushed for something more and better.

Some smaller companies hold bare-bones meetings on the factory floor or in their warehouse, but Berkshire Hathaway's annual meeting is so popular that nearly 40,000 shareholders, analysts, family, friends, and news teams attended in 2010. The basement of the convention center becomes one big Berkshire Hathaway shopping mall, with employee discounts on the many products of the holding companies. How about Fruit of the Loom T-shirts for $2? A Dairy Queen Dilly Bar for $1? You can even buy a modular home at a terrific price.

Thousands of people stick around for the question and answer period following the formal annual meeting. Chairman Warren Buffett and Vice Chairman Charlie Munger sometimes field questions about the company, the economy, and the future of the world for up to six hours.

Michelle Leder, who writes the Footnoted blog, admits that it is not easy for shareholders to effect change, but she encourages them to try. She reported on Morgan Stanley's 2008 annual meeting, after the company wrote off $9.5 billion in subprime mortgages and posted a loss of more than $3 billion for the third quarter of 2007 alone. Leder was surprised at how few questions were posed to the CEO and to the directors. She says she would have asked, "Where were you guys? Why were you asleep at the wheel? Why weren't you warning us beforehand? Why are you still paying out huge chunks of change for what can charitably be called mediocre performance?"[11]

She has a point. As long as shareholders never ask the questions, management will never worry about the answers.

Participatory capitalism can be exciting, but keep this in mind—the Internal Revenue Service does not allow a tax write-off to travel to an annual meeting as an investment expense. So forget about buying a few shares of Hawaiian Electric Industries just for a trip to the tropics or shares in Walt Disney to write off a trip to Orlando.

New and Old Regulations

Many corporate leaders battle government regulations, saying that the rules are oppressive and the high cost of compliance makes them uncompetitive in the world. "Although implementing corporate governance best practices would result in additional operating costs," wrote Jorge E. Guerra in *The CPA Journal* in 2004, "I must emphasize that good corporate governance is not an option but an obligation, if shareholder interest is to be protected. Compliance costs are only a small fraction of the gargantuan losses suffered by stockholders who invested in companies whose shares became worthless because they did not comply with good corporate governance practices. Stockholders of Enron and WorldCom suffered losses of more than $100 billion, while even the most aggressive estimates of Sarbanes–Oxley compliance costs amount to less than $5 billion."[12]

In addition to holding corporations to a higher standard than in the past, Bogle says the government should apply a federal standard of fiduciary duty to institutional money managers. This would force mutual fund and pension fund and other institutional managers, who tend to hold large blocks of shares, to use their stock holdings as a cudgel to demand that directors and executives of corporations honor their responsibilities to owners.

"We need Congress to pass a law establishing the basic principle that money managers are there to serve their shareholders," Bogle said. "And the second part of the demand is that fiduciaries act with due diligence and high professional standards. That doesn't seem to be too much to ask."[13]

Bogle also calls for corporate executives to behave with greater integrity. "Regulation alone will not be sufficient to correct these gross abuses, for the self-interest of our agents, abetted by powerful and well-financed lobbyists—paid for, finally, by the very corporate and mutual fund shareholders whom new regulations are designed to serve. There are few regulations that smart, motivated targets cannot evade."[14]

There is another advantage to insisting on extreme honesty and integrity in the financial fields and that is to preserve the United States as a safe haven for money. For hundreds of years investors from all over the world have been willing to buy U.S. stocks, bonds, and mutual funds because they trusted the regulatory system. The entire U.S. economy benefits from a good reputation.

Signs of Corporate Trouble

Many investors felt both appalled and helpless in the face of the out-landish salaries and bonuses paid to employees on Wall Street before the crash of 2007–8. In 1980 the compensation of the typical chief executive of a U.S. corporation was forty-two times the average worker's salary. By 2010, typical CEO compensation had rocketed to four hundred times the average worker's salary.[15]

Investors were baffled when the bonuses resumed even before investors had recouped huge losses in retirement and other accounts and unemployment reached epic proportions. "Despite the collapse in corporate earnings during the recent financial crisis," wrote Bogle, "there are few signs that executive compensation has been significantly affected."[16]

Wall Street salaries were just as bloated. Bonuses there grew 17 percent in 2009 to a total of $20.3 billion, as many investment banks that had been bailed out by taxpayers reported blowout profits.[17]

How could such compensation be justified? the public asked. Banks and other financial institutions insisted that to keep good employees, the high salaries were necessary. They never explained where else, in such a poor economy, these people would find employment. Considering how many of these companies had failed and how tenuous the operations of others like them had become, job openings in that industry were hard to find. There were more people to fill positions than jobs that were available.

It has always been difficult for shareholders to know how much top executives earn and to determine exactly how much top management *should* earn. Clearly, strong, talented, and ethical management is worth paying for. Compensation committees and consultants aren't much help. They look to average salaries and benefits in the business, but averages can quite easily be driven beyond reason by widespread, aggressive, and egregious demands for compensation.

Financial reform passed in 2010 gives shareholders greater input to executive compensation. The SEC also voted to propose better disclosure of executive compensation at public companies in their proxy statements, and approved a New York Stock Exchange rule change to prohibit brokers from voting proxies in corporate elections without instructions from their customers. It remains to be seen if these measures are enough to contain abuses.

Economist Ravi Nagarajan stresses the importance of "trustworthy" management. "Often investors examine 10K reports but fail to examine the proxy statement detailing executive compensation practices. This can be a warning sign when examining any company, but is particularly important for NCAV [net current asset value] scenarios."[18]

Buried in the Footnotes

A major source of hidden information about corporate activities can be found in the footnotes of Securities and Exchange Commission filings. By reading footnotes you might have learned that the chief executive of a self-named and self-founded corporation was paying herself millions of dollars as a retention fee. In other words, she was granting herself a bonus not to leave her own company. You could also find out which CEOs are using corporate jets and helicopters for personal travel, including ferrying children to school. For example, in 2008 the share price of Abercrombie & Fitch declined around 70 percent, but the chief executive's personal travel expenses increased by 60 percent over the previous year. That somehow seems incongruous.

Many companies fully disclose salaries, bonuses, and perks, but this information is found in complicated formulations, tucked into small-print footnotes or addenda to the basic material. Information on compensation should be reported all in one place and in plain English. Just like taxpayers, what investors need most is simplification.

Chapter 9

Stock Picking

POSP will be the theme that I highlight—Plain Old Stock Picking.[1]

MARIO GABELLI BLOG, JANUARY 21, 2009

This is where the rubber meets the road, where the theories, academic studies, and raw reasoning are tested. This is the moment. This is where we become more intimate participants in the great capitalist economic system. This is the way we choose shares to buy in public companies. This is game day.

As you think about your investment strategy, keep these words of wisdom in mind:

From Benjamin Graham, more than fifty years ago: "Investors do not make mistakes, or bad mistakes, in buying good stocks at fair prices. They make their serious mistakes by buying poor stocks, particularly the ones that are pushed for various reasons, and sometimes—in fact, very frequently—they make mistakes by buying good stocks in the upper reaches of bull markets."[2]

From Warren Buffett: An education in investing, he says, "requires only two courses: How to Value a Business and How to Think About Markets. You don't have to know how to value all businesses. Start with a small circle of competence, businesses you can understand."[3] Start with an industry in which you already have experience or know something about and expand your circle from there.

From William O'Neil: Although he is sometimes seen as a chartist and short-term investor, O'Neil pays a lot of attention to the fundamentals before buying an equity. "We know that earnings are the driving force," says O'Neil. "We want accelerating earnings, supported by strong sales, a high return on investment—50 percent—and a high pre-tax profit margin. We also want to see that this company has a product that is different, has repeat sales, is superior to others in its space. After putting all the fundamentals together, we go to the behavior of the stock itself. But if something is missing in fundamentals, we don't play."

From David Iben: Iben repeats the mantra of many value investors: Past performance is not a reliable indicator of future performance. Logic is more important. He gives this example of illogical thought. "If you were thinking about getting life insurance, you could use as proof that for 52 years, not one single day, did I die. That would suggest you're not going to die."

More from Iben: Even in bad times, some stocks come up winners. "The stocks of those entities that are able to effectively manage through the crises should prove to be tremendous investments," contends Iben. "The large well-capitalized companies have a once-per-generation opportunity to acquire great franchises at distressed prices."[4]

When buying shares on the stock exchanges, consider the following points as reasons for your purchases:

- Stick to your investment goals. If you seek high growth, look to future prospects. If you require income, consider the quality of the company and the dividend record. Always seek the best way to preserve capital.

- Use the balance sheet and income statement to establish the upper and lower price parameters for a specific stock. Intrinsic value fluctuates somewhere between the asset value and a conservative multiple of earnings. Traditionally a nicely valued stock will sell for 20 times earnings or less. However, quality stocks with plenty of growth ahead may sell for higher multiples.

- Shy away from too much debt. Poorly capitalized enterprises are marked by a relatively large amount of senior securities and debt, as compared with a small issue of common stock.

- Identify a margin of safety such as a best-selling product that everyone needs. Or you might select a company that is first, second, or third in its industry. Such companies are more likely to survive, and even expand, when the economy is bleak.

- Measure the qualitative factors. Statistics and numbers might be deceptive, but by stepping back and looking at who runs the company, what the company does, where it does business, and other factors, you will have a better idea of why you should or should not buy it.

Building Your Own Screen

There are a great many Internet tools that allow investors to search for stocks with certain characteristics. Almost all of the Internet portals such as AOL, MSN, Yahoo!, Google, and others have sections on money and investing. E-Trade, Charles Schwab, TD Ameritrade, and other brokerages provide enormous online help. If you want to do your own research and analysis, these sites offer excellent tools for doing so.

Graham once constructed a list of ten attributes of undervalued shares. It is unrealistic to expect that any company's shares match all ten traits. Graham figured that any stock that met seven of the ten has an adequate margin of safety. Just remember that these are guidelines. They can be used as a screen to find deeply discounted stocks and can be modified to locate stocks to meet specific goals.

Items 1 through 5 pertain to risk; 6 and 7 measure financial soundness; 8 through 10 indicate a history of stable earnings. Most of the ratios used to make these calculations are readily available and the formulas for most are also listed at the end of chapter 6.

1. An earnings-to-price yield (reverse of P/E ratio) that is double the AAA bond yield. If the AAA bond yield is 4 percent, the earnings yield should be 8 percent.

2. A price-to-earnings ratio that is four tenths of the highest average P/E ratio achieved by the shares in the most recent years.

3. A dividend yield of two thirds the AAA bond yields.

4. A share price of two thirds the tangible book value per share. In inflationary times, this item should be given extra weight.

5. A stock with two thirds the net current asset value or the net quick liquidation value. This was among the earliest techniques Graham used. It is a worst case scenario, estimating the amount a company would sell for if it had to immediately go out of business.

6. Total debt that is lower than the tangible book value.

7. A current ratio of two or more. This is a measure of liquidity, or a company's ability to pay its debts from its income.

8. Total debt of no more than the net quick liquidation value.

9. Earnings that have doubled in the most recent ten years. Equities that either don't pay a dividend or are not currently profitable will be automatically eliminated.

10. Earnings that have declined no more than 5 percent in two of the past ten years.[5]

To build a screen for an income portfolio:

- Insist that the stock comply with Rule 3.

- Place special emphasis on criteria 1 through 7.

For a high-growth portfolio:

- Ignore Rule 3.

- Give light weighting to Rules 4, 5, and 6.

- Place heavy emphasis on Rules 9 and 10.

Screening for Low-Maintenance Stocks

Those who aim to balance safety and appreciation may ignore Rule 3 and focus on items 1 through 5, plus items 9 and 10. However, in *The Intelligent Investor*, Graham laid out seven simple requirements for a company to be included in a defensive, conservative investment plan:

■ Adequate size. By today's standards that would be a company with around $200 million annual sales and at least $100 million in assets.

■ A strong financial condition shown by a 2-to-1 current ratio.

■ Twenty years of continuous dividend payment.

■ No earnings deficit for at least a decade.

■ Earnings growth of at least 33.3 percent over the prior ten years.

■ A share price of no more than 1.5 times net asset value.

■ A share price of no more than 15 times average earnings for the past three years.

While this strategy eliminates almost every fast-paced growth issue, it is calculated to ensure stability and growth over long periods of time. This is a "buy and hold" portfolio made up of stocks that plod steadily along, seldom at the head of the herd in a bull market. These same stocks tend to avoid the plunge when the bull dashes off a cliff.

A Possibly Overvalued Stock

This heading includes the word "possibly," because if you feel certain your shares are overvalued, you always should consider selling them and reinvesting the money in an undervalued issue. It is the shares that are overvalued but not yet at a price that makes it obvious that keep you awake at night. For most investors, the decision to sell stocks is more difficult than the decision to buy. If the company has done well and the price has appreciated nicely, there is a tendency to fall in love with the stock. It seems to be an Olympian security, and we want to believe it can run forever. If the shares have done poorly, we tend to hang on, hoping that things will improve. Change is always just around the corner.

The characteristics that describe an overblown stock market may also apply to specific shares. Additionally, when reevaluating holdings look for these signs of trouble:

- High executive salaries and bonuses

- Overly generous compensation for boards of directors

- Constant disputes between management and auditors

- Frequent change of auditors

- Repeatedly switching from one form of depreciation to another

When a stock or a portfolio is overvalued you can use a stop loss order, hedge, or sell. The decisions around selling shares will be addressed in chapter 10.

Hedging

Hedging, or the buying of an asset with an opposite correlation to an initial investment, is a classic technique for offsetting or reducing the risk presented by negative events. Farmers use hedging to protect themselves against the low price of corn; oil companies and public utilities hedge against a disruption in the oil supply. Large international firms hedge currencies needed to conduct business abroad. (Don't confuse hedging with hedge funds, which are private investment companies that should but do not always hedge.)

There are many different ways to hedge, but the process basically requires the purchase of a second asset with a negative correlation to the first. If the hedged security moves lower, the hedge moves in the opposite direction and can be sold at a profit to minimize the investor's loss.

Options have become the favored hedging instrument for investors all over the world, particularly when hedging stock portfolios.

For small and individual investors, hedging may appear to be profitable when used sparingly and effectively. But hedging is usually so expensive that the reduced risk comes with reduced returns. For this reason, many long-term value investors do not hedge.

Defensive Stocks

If conditions have dictated the sale of a security and yet the economic outlook is unpredictable, investors can stay in the market by taking refuge in defensive stocks. This is an especially useful strategy for those who are a number of years from needing to use their investment funds. Defensive stocks tend to weather economic storms well, and if they have been impacted, they often rebound faster. These companies include those in the essential industries such as public utilities, food and grocery companies, drugmakers, and the like.

If you are within five years of retirement and the market is making you jumpy, you may choose to move more aggressively toward fixed income and guaranteed securities.

The securities are the building blocks of a sound portfolio. In the chapter ahead we will consider ways to put those blocks together to structure a solid, balanced portfolio that can serve an investor for many years.

Guidance for Online Investing

From wherever you happen to be in the world, with the click of a mouse, you can check on the market levels or check the price of your shares. You are able to buy and sell stocks using one of more than one hundred online brokerage houses for as low as $5 per transaction. Online trading is fast, frugal, and fun and it is easy to track an investment portfolio. Many of the online brokerages offer a variety of services, including research reports and various fixed-income securities under their own sponsorship.

While online investing is efficient and popular, the Securities and Exchange Commission warns that online investing brings its own risks. The Internet is an open gate to fraudulent or marginal operations. Investors must know whom they are trading with, what they are buying, and the underlying risks of the investment. And then, trading is so fast that investors should take additional steps to guard against problems.

- Know who you're dealing with. Check out the brokerage house to make sure it is licensed and operating under proper regulatory authority. The Internet is crawling with scams.

- Do not place a market order. Instead, place a limit order to buy or sell at a specific price. A buy limit order can only be executed at the limit price or lower, and a sell limit order can only be executed at the limit price or higher. For example, if you are trying to buy shares in a hot initial public offering that was first offered at $7, but don't want to pay more than $15, place a limit buy order for any price up to $15. This way you won't end up paying $25 for a stock that dives to $5 within hours or days.

- Be aware that online trading isn't always instantaneous. The choke point or point of slow-down may be your own computer or modem, the brokerage's system, or simply heavy traffic on the Internet. There are no SEC regulations that require a trade to be executed within a set period of time. However, if firms promote their speed of execution, they must not exaggerate or fail to tell investors about the possibility of delays.

- If you don't get a quick confirmation, don't assume your order didn't go through. Some investors have mistakenly thought their order had not been executed and placed a second order. They ended up either owning twice as many shares as they wanted or could afford, or selling twice as many shares as they owned. If you have doubts about the status of the order, contact the brokerage for more information.

- If you change your mind about an order, act fast. Orders can only be canceled if they have not been executed. Even if you receive an electronic receipt for the cancellation, don't assume that the cancellation was executed before the transaction was. If in doubt, again, check with your brokerage.

- If you buy a security in a cash account, you must pay for it before selling it. If you buy or sell a stock without paying for it you are "freeriding." There are severe penalties for freeriding because it violates the credit extension provisions of the Federal Reserve Board. Your broker will be required to freeze your account for ninety days. You can still trade while the freeze is in effect, but must fully pay for any purchase on the day you trade.

- If you trade on margin and the account falls below the firm's maintenance margin requirements, your broker can sell your securities without warning you with a margin call. Margin calls are a courtesy, not a requirement. In a rapidly declining market your broker could sell your entire margin account at a substantial loss because the securities in the account have fallen in value and the brokerage house does not want to lose money on the part of the account it financed.

- If a problem occurs, deal with it quickly. There is a limited time in which to take legal action, if that becomes necessary. First, try everything possible to resolve your problem with the online broker. If that fails, gather up your documentation and contact the National Association of Securities Dealers, your state securities administrator, or the Securities and Exchange Commission.

Chapter 10

Portfolio Requirements

As the saying goes, a stock well bought is half sold. I think Ben was an expert in that area.

WALTER SCHLOSS[1]

Benjamin Graham believed that there were two stances for an investor to take when building a securities portfolio. Those who had limited tolerance for risk should be "defensive"; those with the time and temperament should be "enterprising." Defensive investors should be protecting their assets in the best possible way. By enterprising, Graham meant dedicated investors who could be more adventuresome and creative in their quest for financial growth. Those two simple categories seem easy enough to understand, but we would add a third category, that of the passive, or noninvestor. Those who cannot or choose not to do the homework should park their money in a safe place and do a periodic check to make sure their parking lot is still protected. All other investors will want to structure a portfolio that meets the needs and wants of their lives.

Graham also wrote in *The Intelligent Investor* that it is a misconception that those who cannot afford to take risks must be extremely conservative and therefore are stuck with a lower rate of return. Indeed this may sometimes happen, but it is not an unbreakable rule. Graham said the rate of return instead should depend on the amount of "intelligent effort" the investor is willing to put into the work.

Goals

The principles taught by Graham and used by so many disciples can apply no matter what your investment goals may be. Investors need to think about what they want to accomplish and direct their money in the desired direction.

- Those who need to defer taxes should take full advantage of tax-sheltered accounts such as a company-sponsored plan like a 401(k), a traditional Individual Retirement Account, SEP, etc.

- If you've maximized the allowable depositors for tax-deferred accounts, invest the remainder of your funds in quality securities that you can hold for the longest term possible. If you still need tax relief, consider the various high-quality tax-free bonds that may be available, but only if they surpass the possible after-tax returns from investments in stocks or other types of bonds.

- Those looking for growth without the drag of future taxes can fully utilize a Roth IRA. With a Roth, taxes are paid on the money before it is invested but it builds and is withdrawn later, tax free. You can have a traditional IRA and a Roth IRA at the same time and can make contributions to a Traditional and a Roth IRA in the same year. However, your total annual contribution to either or both IRAs cannot exceed $5,000 per individual in any year. For example, you might contribute $2,500 to a traditional IRA and $2,500 to a Roth IRA in the same year.

- Those who need current income can choose from a wide range of sound, dividend-paying securities or when advantageous, Treasury securities. There are various other types and durations of bonds available, but that's the subject of another entire book. Also, the U.S. Treasury Web site has full information on the securities and how to buy them.

■ It is always tricky to base investments on philosophical principles, either avoiding certain types of enterprises or encouraging them, but many investors feel they cannot invest any other way. Socially responsible investors may seek companies that work on solutions to environmental problems, that shun child labor, or that don't operate in countries with oppressive regimes. This type of investing is not at odds with value principles; in fact they work quite well together. Socially responsible investing simply adds another dimension to the investment process by screening out those companies that don't meet the investor's goals.

■ Historically, common stocks have offered the best opportunity for staying ahead of inflation and growing wealth. Over a sixty-year period ending in 2009 the total return for the S&P 500 Index grew at an average annualized rate of 9.2 percent.

Investing, as we've said before, involves a large amount of common sense and a smaller amount of greed. "Nowhere does it say that investors should strive to make every last dollar of potential profit," says Seth Klarman. "Consideration of risk must never take a backseat to return."[2]

Beating the Dow

Many money managers claim triumph if they beat the S&P 500 or the DJIA, even if it's only by a portion of a point. If you are only matching an index fund—and be sure to average trading costs into the mix—you may as well buy index funds and give yourself less stress and more free time. On the other hand, investment goals should be reasonable, and allow for years of good performance and years of poor performance. At the very minimum, investors should aim to beat the rate of inflation with their investment returns. This way spending power is growing faster than it is dissipating, making your gains real ones. Although it varies from year to year, inflation has averaged about 3 percent a year for several decades.

- If, over time, you are beating inflation with a couple of points to spare, you are doing well. In times of a healthy bull market, stock market investments very likely will bring greater returns than inflation, which is cause for celebration.

- As a general rule, the average sales growth rate for companies represented in the portfolio should be 10 percent.

The Classic Conservative

Early on, when Buffett was running Buffett Limited Partnership, his critics said that he could not be considered a conservative investor because his choices were too unconventional. Somehow the critics were interchanging the two words, conservative and conventional.

"It is unquestionably true that other investment companies have their money more conventionally invested than we do," Buffett wrote to his investors. "To many people, conventionality is indistinguishable from conservatism."

This is wrongheaded, he claimed. "Truly conservative actions arise from intelligent hypotheses, correct facts, and sound reasoning. These qualities may lead to conventional acts, but there have been many times when they have led to unorthodoxy."[3]

This concept is especially difficult to practice but essential to remember during times of fear and uncertainty. Stick to one of Graham's basic principles—think for yourself. Don't follow the crowd.

Old-fashioned Dollar Cost Averaging

Dollar cost averaging is a simple, traditional concept that passive investors use to navigate the uncertainties of the stock market. Often DCA is considered the opposite of lump sum investing. Say you have $10,000 to put into the stock market. Rather than investing it all at once, you divide it into segments and buy shares at a regular interval over time. For example, you may divide it into five parts and buy 2,000 shares each month for five months. The argument goes that in this way you are more likely to pay the average price for a stock over time rather than risk buying at a high price.

This technique often is suggested as a way to establish simplicity and discipline when investing.

Many investors use dollar cost averaging with the idea that it brings superior results and protection from market swings. While saving and investing your money consistently over time is sure to build wealth, classic dollar cost averaging may not give you the advantages and protection you are aiming for.

"Ever since the landmark article by Constantinides (1979), the academic literature has been decrying the inefficiency of the investment strategy known as dollar-cost averaging (DCA)," writes Professor Moshe A. Milevsky. "In fact, despite more than twenty years of damning evidence, DCA remains as popular as ever amongst the press and individual investors."[4]

The method has several drawbacks:

- It often ignores transaction fees, which can be substantial.

- Studies indicate that dollar cost averaging tends to bring lower returns overall. Dollar cost averagers always face a statistical headwind by choosing to invest tomorrow rather than today, even though on average tomorrow's prices are likely to be higher.

- It does not significantly reduce risk when compared with other strategies because the market trends upward over time.

If you are willing to do some work and pay attention to market conditions, a reverse variation on dollar cost averaging may serve you wonderfully well. First, choose a high-quality stock that meets all the criteria of a value investment and buy the number of shares that fit your pocketbook and portfolio requirements for diversification. As long as your stock and the market are trending upward (despite the normal market swings), hold it and watch it. If the market seems to be overheated and becomes unusually volatile, or if your shares are still appreciating but you believe they may be overvalued, systematically begin selling a portion of the holdings. Again, you may sell a percentage, say one fourth, and monitor the situation. If the risk persists, sell another fourth, and so on. Once again, consider the transaction costs when planning such a strategy.

You may also use dollar cost averaging to advantage when you spot a company that is fundamentally sound but in temporary trouble that pummels its share price. For example, the shares of a major oil company may be declining due to disruptions in the oil supply market, but you believe that the company has reserves and resources to emerge whole and profitable. Rather than try to guess the bottom of the decline, buy a set number of shares each month while the price is retreating. When the company rebounds from its brief setback the price appreciation can be very quick, and you will be positioned to profit from it.

Once the security is on a solid upward path, you would stop buying it and hold on for the long term or set a price target for a possible sale. And when would that be? Some investors set a target when the shares have appreciated by a certain percentage, say 50 percent. However, this sometimes leads to unloading a wonderful, long-term gainer. Most often you would sell when the price-to-earnings and price-to-book ratios have soared above a reasonable or normal range for that stock and for its industry.

Diversification

"You can't always predict the future," says Charles Brandes. "That's why you have a diversified portfolio."

While Brandes's words are true, in the crash of 2007–8 we learned that diversification—all by itself—isn't adequate protection. Nearly all segments of the market were damaged. And yet, some were battered less than others, and some stocks within each category survived better than their counterparts. If we could accurately identify winners every time, as Brandes suggests, diversification would be unnecessary. We would just buy one stock and stick with it. Since few investors have a reliable crystal ball allowing them to peer into the future, diversification lends balance and stability to a portfolio of carefully chosen securities that offer a margin of safety:

▪ Diversification smooths out much of the stock market's turbulence when measured by total return. In most markets stocks do not move in unison. According to the Rule of Five, one in five of your carefully selected stocks will encounter unforeseen trouble and tank, three will more or less perform as expected, and one will be an outlier in the best sense. Peter Lynch described the fifth stock as the "ten-bagger." This refers to an investment that becomes worth ten times its original purchase price. Lynch borrowed the term from baseball, where "bag" is slang for "base" and extra-base hits such as doubles, triples, and home runs are colloquially called two-, three-, or four-baggers. Ten-bagger stocks hit the ball out of the park. Diversification increases the chances of finding the ten-bagger that makes up for the strikeouts and ordinary performers.

- Diversification into different asset classes affords protection against interest rate shifts, difficult housing markets, oil crises, and other periodic but unpredictable disruptions. This is why mutual fund manager David Iben says it is wise to own some gold and real estate for investment purposes.

- Global diversification not only expands the investment universe, it also guards against international currency swings.

The First Rule of Diversification

Graham recommended two simple approaches to structuring an investment portfolio. The first rule balances stocks versus fixed-income securities within the portfolio. The second rule calls for a sufficient number of different shareholdings so that one or two surprisingly bad performances don't sink the entire portfolio.

Those following the first rule would have had at least some small level of protection in 2007–8.

According to this theory, you should distribute your investments between stocks and bonds, with 25 to 75 percent of the funds in bonds, depending on interest rates. When high rates are available in high-quality bonds, the portfolio may hold 75 percent of interest-earning investments.

When bond qualities and interest rates are low, stocks should represent a higher proportion of the portfolio, although never more than 75 percent. And at the bottom of the market when excellent companies are selling for low prices, the portfolio would be laden with stocks.

Other factors also influence the mix:

■ Younger investors with good future earnings ability might have as much as 75 percent of their money in the stock market. The older the investor, the lower the percentage of funds in stocks. At a certain age, safety trumps growth. John Bogle, who is in his seventies, recently said he has 75 percent of his assets in bonds.

■ Any money that you will need to use in three years or less should be held in a liquid, interest-bearing account of some type. A college fund, money saved for a wedding, or the down payment for a home would fall into this category. A money market fund or certificate of deposit with an appropriate maturity would do the job.

Again, it is best not to obsess too much about the exact percentages. Buffett, who likes to compare investing to farming, might say: plant it, protect it, let it grow, and then harvest when the time is right.

Is Cash Trash?

Traditionally cash and cash equivalents have provided safety of capital, have been a storehouse of wealth, and at times when interest rates run high have been a source of superior return. In the future, however, fixed investments should be handled with care. Investors should hold as little cash as their lives and circumstances allow.

For those who need to use funds within three years, inflation isn't such a critical issue. Those with a longer investment timeline must be aware of the erosion of their purchasing power. Inflation is always a lurking enemy for investors. If your money earns a return smaller than the rate of inflation, you continually lose purchasing power. Your dollar is gradually worth less and less.

Changes in the strength of the dollar in the twenty-first century, plus the strong likelihood of inflation, says Buffett, put cash in a precarious position. "Cash is a terrible investment. I say it again in the [2009] annual report. If they think cash is king, people are wrong. We're following policies over time that will make currency denominated investments worth less. We can't bet on the speed, but we can bet on direction."

Because of long and costly wars, the various economic recovery packages, coupled with reduced tax revenues due to high unemployment, government spending is sure to increase. When the government prints more money to cover its spending, inflationary times follow. How should an investor cope with inflation?

- Again, despite the market's erratic behavior over the past decade, well-purchased stocks still offer the best protection against the erosion of money.

- In times of expected inflation, investors should consider various alternatives including real estate. Gold, a traditional hedge against inflation, has had such a remarkable run in the first decade of the twenty-first century that it is most likely overpriced, but in normal times gold is worth considering as a storehouse of value and hedge against inflation.

As dire as the anticash warnings are, investors need enough spare cash on hand for their personal rainy-day fund, and also to take advantage of investment bargains as they pop up.

The Second Rule of Diversification

Buffett often says that life would be simply grand if you could find one great company and hold nothing more. It would be easy and effective. That might happen in an ideal world, not in a realistic one. Even the triad that runs Google, founders Larry Page and Sergey Brin and chief executive officer Eric Schmidt, sells a small portion of their Google shares each year. They are systematically taking profits and presumably investing the money elsewhere to spread the risk of being too heavily weighted in Google.

Following the crash of 1929, Benjamin Graham held a very large variety of shares in his portfolio. He was finding a great many deeply undervalued shares, but the economy dripped with uncertainty and many companies operated in tenuous circumstances. Graham found safety in numbers. Typically, he would want a minimum of thirty stocks in a portfolio: the deeper the discount of the purchase price of the shares, the more shares he would want to hold.

"One of the mainstays of our operations was the rather undiscriminating purchase of common stocks at a price below their net-current-asset value," he explained, "and later, sale, typically at prices to yield a profit of 20 percent or more per annum. Our portfolio often included more than 100 of such bargain issues at a given time; fully 90 percent of these returned satisfactory profits over three and one-half decades."[5]

Buffett warns that holding too many different stocks means you don't get to know any of them very well. "Every new investment decision should be measured against what you already own. We measure every new investment against buying more Coca-Cola. You should only buy if you like the new stock more than everything else that you own. The problem for most people is that it requires you to know what you own. If you own too many stocks, you can't possibly know them all. This is one of the most important investment lessons, and one of the easiest for an individual to follow, but often overlooked."[6]

Even so, as far as returns are concerned, there is no upper limit to the number of shares you might want to hold. "Returns are not diluted by an increased number of portfolio issues—so long as strict value criteria are followed,"[7] notes Charles Brandes.

Few of us are able to study and track as many as one hundred different securities. Often as few as ten stocks is an adequate beginning number, especially when an investment pool is small, perhaps $10,000 or less. The number of stocks you own can expand as experience and resources increase.

Industry Groups

Investors are sometimes advised to choose the best industry groups in terms of the current economy, then pick the lowest priced, strongest operation within that group. David Iben of Tradewinds funds says to look for good businesses in industries that meet the needs of a growing middle class around the world, such as food, energy, and telecommunications. Those industries will invariably have barriers to entry and allow a healthy return on capital.

Buffett in recent years has thought along similar lines as Iben. In his 2009 letter to shareholders he wrote, "Our BNSF [railroad]operation, it should be noted, has certain important economic characteristics that resemble those of our electric utilities. In both cases, we provide fundamental services that are, and will remain, essential to the economic well-being of our customers."[8]

Iben invests in technology stocks, but only when he can do appropriate analysis on them. "But we sidestep the high-tech franchises that are the latest and greatest. All too often they're gone next year."

Going Global

As recently as the late twentieth century Buffett and other major U.S. investors shunned foreign investments. Buffett felt that he understood the rules of domestic exchanges and that there were so many good U.S. companies that shopping abroad was unnecessary. That time is now several decades behind us. When the Italian giant Fiat owns 20 percent of Chrysler Corp., Kraft Foods owns the legendary British candy maker Cadbury, and Berkshire Hathaway owns 10 percent of the Chinese electric car company BYD Auto and most of the Israeli manufacturer Iscar Metalworking Companies (which itself owns the Japanese company Tungaloy), how can we not think of the business world as a big international family?

It now is essential to include foreign holdings in a portfolio, partly because much of the strongest economic growth is taking place abroad and partly because the U.S. dollar has been losing purchasing power in the world. Owning foreign stocks often balances out swings in the U.S. stock markets, although in 2007–8, most foreign markets suffered right along with Americans. Yet there were countries such as Brazil, China, Germany, and Canada with stable governments, growing economies, and very low national debt that endured the crisis well.

David Iben especially likes to find investments in smaller countries that are in the early stages of economic development. "Emerging markets should do well over time," Iben believes. "They still need to add infrastructure and should continue to develop their consumer economies. Importantly, unlike the developed economies, India and China have the reserves to fund their capital spending needs."[9]

Indeed, in 2009 emerging market funds soared in value. The T. Rowe Price Emerging Europe & Mediterranean Fund, for instance, was up 113 percent that year.

There are three ways to participate in the global market:

- By investing in a closed-end global fund.

- Through foreign companies traded on a U.S. exchange as an American depositary receipt (ADR). There are hundreds of ADR companies including British Petroleum, Telkom Indonesia, and Total, a French oil company.

- By purchasing U.S.-based companies with a strong global presence, such as Kraft, Google, Microsoft, or General Electric. GE operates in one hundred countries and generates more than half its revenues from outside the United States.

South Korea and Mexico are among the most developed of the emerging economies, although the BRICs, a group accounting for more than one fourth of the world's landmass and more than 40 percent of its population, have come center stage.

The BRICs

Arguably Brazil, Russia, India, and China—nicknamed the BRICs— are the most popular current destinations for global investors. It is estimated that by the year 2050 these four countries will be wealthier than most of the current major economic powers.[10] Jim O'Neill, global economist at Goldman Sachs, has predicted that by then China and India will become the world's leading suppliers of manufactured goods and services and Brazil and Russia will be the dominant suppliers of raw materials. These nations together, between the years 2003 and 2009, experienced a 500 percent growth rate, indicating that investors might like to jump aboard.

The leaders of these nations are keenly aware that their economic growth could translate into global political power. They have met twice, first in the summer of 2009 and again in 2010, to discuss the possibilities presented by forming some sort of coalition.

While these countries have modified their political systems to embrace capitalism and have been dynamic and progressive in terms of economic management, investments there are not without risk. The high expectations are based on predictions, and the future isn't always so predictable. Each country also has its own social problems and political uncertainty.

There are a variety of BRIC exchange traded funds based largely on the Dow Jones BRIC 50 Index.

The PIIGS

Following the market crash and worldwide recession that started in 2007, the PIIGS fell into woeful economic circumstances. The countries with such an unflattering acronym are Portugal, Ireland, Italy, Greece, and Spain. For value investors looking to buy $1 worth of assets for 50 cents, the PIIGS represent a special circumstance. When they do recover, the discounted assets may very well rebound with breathtaking speed. Ireland, for example, once was the darling of those betting on the emerging nations. The so-called Celtic Tiger excelled because of money poured into education, infrastructure supported by the European Community, and incentives Ireland itself gave to companies that located operations there. Ireland still has the assets and infrastructure that it built up during that time; it still has a young, educated, bright, and willing workforce; and it is very likely that the government will, in time, work through its problems.

There are funds that focus on each of the emerging economies. The Ireland Fund, take note, is not an investment vehicle; rather it is a charitable fund that uses its resources to support peace and political and social improvements in the country. The New Ireland Fund, however, is a mutual fund made up of Irish securities.

Gold

For thousands of years gold has fascinated and lured investors, and certainly it has had a very strong run in the early twenty-first century. In 1995 gold languished at around $370 per ounce. By mid-2010 it had topped $1,100 per ounce. The price increases slowed down after that, but it didn't appear as though gold would decline in price any time soon.

The Nuveen Fund's David Iben encourages everyone to hold some gold, even at its recent high price, as a hedge against inflation. Historically, notes Iben, an ounce of gold would buy a high-quality man's suit, no matter how low or high inflation was at any given time. "Gold is far from perfect," he says, "but what it has is that it cannot be printed (unlike money)."

Many value investors realize gold's limitations, but invest in it as a practical matter. Buffett acknowledges the importance of gold, but he wants people to put the precious metal in proper perspective: "You can say it is an asset, like art is, but something that doesn't produce anything isn't an investment. Stamps are assets. A farm is an investment. You can speculate in an asset class if you want, but you're only betting against others. As long as the next guy wants it, it's fine." Once others lose interest, the value of the asset dissipates.

Buffett thinks gold will become less important over time. Most investors agree on one point: gold is not an investment in the real sense because it produces no earnings. However, it can be useful as a storehouse of value. Owning a small amount of gold, around 5 percent of total holdings, is a prudent move.

Iben prefers gold mining stocks to actual physical gold. He seeks companies that hold large stores of gold in the ground and that are extracting it slowly. He calculates the company's total cost of gold per share using the company's market value, debt, capital-spending needs, and operating costs. In this way he determines whether the company can profitably mine and sell the gold. If there is a margin of safety, he stakes a claim.

"If you have $20 billion of gold sitting in the bank," explains Iben, "ask a couple of people what it is worth and they will say $20 billion. Dig a hole in the ground, cover it up, and people then say it's worth $10 billion. It would take about $3 billion to mine the gold out of the ground. So for $13 billion you get $20 billion worth of gold. That's buying something for 70 cents on the dollar."

Gold coins can be purchased directly from the U.S. Mint but they must be stored and cared for properly. Gold exchange traded funds (GETFs) are another way of buying gold, since it makes it easier to buy, hold, or sell gold equivalents as needed. Typically GETFs charge a 9.4 percent commission for trading plus an annual storage fee. Because GETFs may have a complicated structure and limited regulation, due diligence is necessary.

Just keep this in mind—like any other storehouse of value, gold prices can dive as easily as they soar. Even more important to remember, because gold has an emotional component: gold fever attracts speculators, promoters, and charlatans who seek to separate honest investors from their cash.

Mutual Funds

Mutual funds are convenient, they come in a wide variety of permutations, and with more than fifteen thousand funds to choose from, they have become a staple investment product. However, as a group they often have not performed well and the research and management fees run up the cost of investing. While no-load funds charge no sales commission, they are not free. There is a management fee.

For a number of years, the typical actively managed stock mutual fund has returned approximately 2 percent less per year to shareholders than stock market returns in general.[11] John Bogle, founder of the Vanguard funds, has written an entire book arguing that most investors (including the endowments of nonprofits) would be better off investing in low-cost index funds. Even no-load mutual funds have higher management costs than index funds.

This said, when the market began its 2009 rebound, mutual funds were quick out of the gate. Investors could easily find funds that were up 25 to 35 percent, many value-based funds included. These dramatic gains of course were possible only because the net asset values of the funds had taken such a beating in the previous two years. Even so, nearly two thirds of mutual funds outpaced the Dow. Those individuals who have neither the time nor the interest in studying stocks and the markets may choose to buy value mutual funds, although probing research and comparison is necessary in choosing funds.

Tracking Returns

There are so many effective programs, both low and high tech, for tracking the performance of your stocks. My mother used to keep a simple little notebook with her buy date and purchase price. She faithfully recorded dividends as they arrived. She seldom sold, but on a fairly regular basis she'd check the newspaper financial pages for her share price. If she spotted a disturbing trend, she'd do a little more research. The $10,000 she inherited from her own mother in the 1980s not only helped support her in her retirement, the principal grew about twelvefold in the next twenty-five years. She was like a mother hen clucking over her nest of eggs, but she kept it simple and honest and did a pretty good job.

Today we have a lot more information and many more tools, which in some ways only makes us more confused and anxious. The more we know, the more we worry. Worry doesn't help, but tracking returns and reviewing holdings on a regular basis is a necessity.

"The choice of a common stock is a single act; its ownership is a continuing process," wrote Graham and Dodd. "Certainly there is just as much reason to exercise care and judgment in *being* as *becoming* a stockholder."[12]

The same computer programs used to screen the market for desirable stocks and to analyze securities have components that allow easy recording, tracking, and instant tallying of holdings. These range from online portals such as AOL to services like E-Trade or Charles Schwab. Software programs such as Quicken provide a similar service that easily interfaces with tax preparation software. Those with a tendency to be nervous about stocks should resist the temptation to look into their holdings on a daily basis. Portfolios should be reviewed at least annually, quarterly when something unusual is going on.

Knowing When to Sell

Buffett has often said that his favorite holding time is forever. He's shown this increasingly in the past decade when he buys entire companies rather than just a position in a stock. Once the companies are a subsidiary of Berkshire Hathaway, he's only concerned with profitability and cash generation, not with stock market gyrations. Buffett's approach has evolved as Berkshire grew larger and certainly is not a viable strategy for the rest of us. Still, we can appreciate Buffett's advice to never sell a stock without a good reason to do so.

Knowing when to sell is as important as knowing when to buy. There are multiple reasons you might need or want to sell, and once there is a clear motivation to get out of a stock, don't hesitate to do so. Some reasons to sell are personal:

- You may have reached your risk tolerance. Your stocks are keeping you awake at night.

- You need cash for some unexpected opportunity or the rainy day has arrived and you have an unexpected expense.

- You may be at or near achieving your financial goal. You are ready to buy that house; your child is off to college; you are retiring.

- As you draw nearer to the time of needing your funds, you will want to shift more of your assets into those producing a guaranteed income.

Other reasons are market driven and equally valid:

- The stock has done so well that your portfolio is now out of balance. If you become too heavily weighted in an industry that has become overly popular with investors, it may be smart to rebalance. Graham made it a rule to sell a stock that had appreciated 50 percent or achieved some other target price.

- The company is tanking. You bought the shares because the company had excellent fundamentals, but management, sales, cash flow, or something fundamental has happened to change the picture.

- The stock isn't keeping up. You've found another stock that you expect will bring better returns.

- The dividend is cut or eliminated. Not only do you lose a desired return, this is a red flag that the company expects to generate less income.

Be Slow to Sell

Common sense dictates that you always try to maximize your investment gain by knowing when one of the companies you hold is at risk. On the other hand, don't panic at every unexpected turn of events. Don't eat into your profit by running up a big bill at your brokerage house in commissions through excessive trading. A few clever trades a year will beat a dozen mediocre ones any day.

However, if you believe problems affecting the economy, the market, or your portfolio are long term and will sour your holdings, be ready to solidify your profits.

Knowing How Much to Sell

If you have a good gain in a stock and you still like the fundamentals, consider taking only part of it off the table—say 50 percent—and taking your profit, while letting the remainder continue to grow. This way you lock in a certain level of profit and you can bail on the rest of it when it starts to slide.

While taxes are a factor when it comes to overall return, remember that the point of investing is to make money. Capital gains are something you want, although it increases your return to keep them at a minimum. If you hold your shares for at least a year you get a break on capital gains taxes. After that time most people will pay taxes at 20 percent. Losses also offset capital gains from other sales, such as a mutual fund distribution. Up to $3,000 of net losses can be deducted against other kinds of income.

Once he made the decision to sell, Graham then strove to replace the shares with a new stock with the potential of enhancing his portfolio performance.

Investing for Income

The Internet's Motley Fool calls dividends "The Secret to Growth You Can Count On." In earlier chapters we described dividends as one more place to find a margin of safety. For investors who want to be in the stock market but also need income, dividends provide an interesting and delightful answer.

In the run-up to the 2007 correction, dividend yields on the DJIA were so low that investors treated them with disdain. They represented nothing more than a coincidental sidelight to growth. By late 2008 and early 2009, sneers had turned to respect. The average yield on dividend-paying stocks was above 5 percent, which was 1 percent to 1.5 percent higher than investors could earn in bonds. Furthermore, unlike bonds, dividends have the potential to increase over time, as does the price of the underlying share.

Bond fund managers try to counteract this lack of growth with timing and diversity, but they are limited in what they can do.

Writing for the Motley Fool Web site, Selena Maranjian explained it this way: McDonald's, in mid-2009, was paying $2 a year per share in dividends. "That's a 3.6 percent dividend yield if you buy now . . . but I bought it nearly three years ago, when the price was lower, and that gives me a 5.5 percent yield on my cost," she wrote. "If McDonald's hikes its dividends by 12 percent per year on average, in 12 years it would be paying out nearly $8 per share, giving me a 21 percent yield. In just 15 years, my effective yield would be a whopping 30 percent! And this is all separate from whether or not the stock itself appreciates."[13]

Nevertheless, dividend-paying securities have risks of their own, mainly that the dividend may decrease or be canceled entirely. The risk is greater when the dividend yield seems too generous to be true. The unusually high dividend yield may reflect an unnaturally low share price.

Take precautions against this happening by checking to see if a company's future earnings are likely to support ongoing dividends. Dig around for companies with relatively little debt, healthy cash reserves (found on the balance sheet), and growing revenue, income, and profit margins. Be circumspect if the accounts receivable or inventories are growing faster than sales.

When evaluating the performance of your stock portfolio, keep in mind that total return is share price increase plus dividends.

Reinvesting Dividends

If you don't need current income, you can enroll in a company's dividend reinvestment program and, with no time expended on your part, buy new shares every time dividends are declared. Not only are you dollar cost averaging at low cost and little effort, you most often see your dividends compounding nicely.

Many companies offer a dividend reinvestment program (DRIP), which involves automatic reinvestment of dividends in more company stocks. Investors can enroll in such a program after purchasing a minimum number of shares.

While enrolled in a DRIP the investor does not receive dividends as cash; instead, the dividends are directly reinvested in the underlying equity. This permits the dividends to be immediately invested for the purpose of price appreciation and compounding, without going through a broker or waiting to accumulate enough money to buy a full share of stock. The investor must still pay taxes each year on the dividend income even if it is reinvested.

Some DRIPs charge no commission for reinvesting while others assess fees or proportional commissions.

The share price of the stock purchased in the plan is based on the average cost of the shares purchased by the company during a specific previous period.

Value investors should not participate in a DRIP or use dollar cost averaging when a stock is overvalued. At that point, you must decide whether to hold the stock for its dividend, or to sell, take the profit, and search for another undervalued company with a suitable dividend. Often it is better to sell and look for the next big bargain.

Among the familiar companies listed in the S&P 500 that offer DRIPs are the New York Times Co., Nike, Norfolk Southern Corp., and Northrop Grumman Corp.

The Best Overall Strategy

Robert Maynard, chief investment officer for the Public Employee Retirement System of Idaho (PERSI), took charge of that fund in 1992. When he took over, PERSI was ranked almost dead last for its one-, five-, and ten-year returns. Maynard, who believes in following a simple investment strategy, turned the $9 billion (in assets) fund around.

By mid-2009 PERSI's one-, five-, and ten-year performances ranked in the thirty-third, tenth, and eighteenth percentiles, respectively.

He steers clear of leverage, market timing, complex strategies, and exotic asset classes such as the tricks hedge funds utilize to push for extra marginal return. Those practices, he finds, put funds in danger when the markets get really bumpy.

"A conventional approach prefers the goal of simply staying in the game during calm times in return for much higher chances of survival and avoiding disaster during the wild and turbulent times," says Maynard.[14]

Maynard sees things this way: ". . . one can construct a portfolio with the basic goal of squeezing extra, marginal returns out of the mild periods or one can structure a portfolio with the basic goal of surviving shorter turbulent times in order to reach the calmer 10-plus year time frames. It is difficult, if not impossible, to have both goals at once."[15]

Chapter 11

Special Circumstances

Curiosity is one of the permanent and certain characteristics
of a vigorous mind.

SAMUEL JOHNSON

S pecial investment circumstances are among the most confusing and risky of all stock market investments, and we always see more of them in troubled times. But as fate would have it—with careful analysis and sound judgment—special circumstances can be among the most lucrative and entertaining ways of building wealth. They can pop up at almost any time and in many different places. They include initial public offerings, mergers and acquisitions, bankruptcy plays, convertibles and warrants, and the shares of seriously distressed companies.

Generally only the most experienced investors should respond to special circumstances, but this isn't always the case.

Let's say you work at Company A, an established, profitable, employee-owned high-tech enterprise and have the opportunity to buy additional shares. You know the shares have appreciated steadily, that the future looks bright for your company's products and the company may even go public some day.

Or perhaps you are employed at Company B, a start-up with a game-changing new product in an industry that you understand very well. The company is now going public and you can participate.

The situation at Company B may be fraught with more investment peril than that at Company A, but both are exploding with opportunity. In either case you are working within what Warren Buffett calls your "circle of competence." Your experience in the industry, your familiarity with the technology, and your knowledge of management all come into play.

Special circumstances call for a cool head, restraint, and at times, amending or expanding your investment rules. For Graham, the original opportunity to buy GEICO represented a special circumstance. During his career Buffett has found many special circumstances, especially as Berkshire Hathaway grew and business executives sought him out as a buyer or a savior in unusual situations.

Initial Public Offerings

Investors tend to react to the initial public offerings (IPOs) of a young and frisky company the same way 1849 gold miners responded to news of a fresh strike up the hill. The rush is on. The stories of those who got rich quick from Microsoft, Google, and a dozen other stars lure investors into the mix. In the majority of IPOs, success is not automatic. Only a few people become millionaires. The initial shares often are sold at a high price, which does not hold for long. It can then take years before the share price returns to the IPO level.

In a study of 2,895 IPOs between 1968 and 1998, the average annualized returns were a horrifying negative 45 percent. Many IPOs, despite so much front-end optimism, just flat-out fail to perform over long periods of time. During the dot-com surge in the late 1990s, numerous companies, including VA Linux and TheGlobe.com, experienced huge first-day run-ups—sometimes 100 percent to 300 percent—but ended up later crashing and leaving investors in the lurch. Yet people who

had the savvy to get in and out fast enough on some of these companies made investing look way too easy. They made the game seem too
exciting to miss.

The whole idea of going public is to raise capital, for the owners to
cash in on their venture capital or their sweat equity, and for all shareholders to enjoy instant liquidity. The money paid by new investors in
exchange for equity ownership in the company should be used to increase
shareholder value through various operational and strategic efforts.

It is tough for individual investors to predict what a fresh issue will do
on its initial day of trading and soon thereafter because usually there is
scant historical data with which to evaluate the company. Not only that, but
most IPOs are of companies going through a transitional growth period,
which adds to the uncertainty regarding the future of the enterprise.

But one thing is fairly clear: a rash of IPOs often signals a high
point in a bull market. Entrepreneurs hope to take their company public at the best possible price, which will bring the maximum amount of
cash into the company.

In 1996 when the dot-com bubble was in its glory there were 675
IPOs. In 2001, after the bubble popped, IPO activity on the major
exchanges was down to 80 in the United States.

Additionally the terrorist attacks on September 11, 2001, reduced
the amount of liquidity in the markets and depressed general economic
activity; it wasn't surprising that 2001–3 saw significant decreases in
public offerings.

After the initial shock of the terrorist attack on Wall Street wore off,
IPO activity gradually resumed. Then 2008 brought a crash in IPO activity worldwide due to the global economic crisis. IPO activity shrank in
the United States to 20 deals in 2008 from a total of 159 the previous year.

Once the downside has been considered, IPOs can present unique
investment opportunities, especially if you are able to buy shares at the

starting price. The following guidelines provide some guidance and protection when wading into the IPO market.

- Dig into the research: Objective, high-quality research on privately held companies is an elusive commodity. Nevertheless, study the company's information, and don't hesitate to scan back several years, reading news releases and any other data posted on financial news or the company's Web site. When a company announces an IPO on a major exchange, there likely will be a flurry of analysis and commentary. Read it all. Troll the Internet for employee comments, industry newsletters articles, and whatever else seems illuminating.

- Be sure to read the prospectus or the SEC's S-1 document: This may be dry reading, but it is an essential step in choosing an IPO investment. The SEC has reviewed the prospectus and will have demanded more disclosure, explanations, and information in places where those elements are thin. In the case of Google the SEC objected when the company declared in the S-1 that a lawsuit by Yahoo! was without merit. The SEC considered this a legal conclusion that Google had no authority to reach. Rather than change the wording, Google eliminated the statement by reaching an out-of-court settlement that gave Yahoo! 2.7 million shares of the company. Because of SEC supervision, IPO documents tend to be conservative, since most companies realize their reputations are in question if they overpromise and underdeliver.

- Favor companies with strong, well-known brokers: Generally, the larger, better-known underwriting firms have the advantage of representing more desirable companies. Unfortunately, it may be difficult for individual investors to get in on a great IPO unless they are major, long-standing investors with the firm.

- Look askance at unsolicited IPO pitches from stockbrokers: This may mean the underwriting company is having trouble selling shares and has embarked on an aggressive sales campaign.

- Check the lock-up period: After a company goes public, insiders cannot sell their shares for a designated period of time. This lock-up period typically runs for ninety days to a year, giving outside investors some measure of protection. If the newly public entity has some secrets or there are surprise developments, insiders are deterred from acting on their knowledge and flipping shares before the public catches on. Some companies set extra-long lock-up periods to inspire confidence in the offering. This means that if you are checking for insider sales and haven't seen any for a newly listed company, it isn't necessarily a good omen. The insiders may simply be waiting for the lock-up period to end to unload shares as quickly as they can legally do so.

- Look carefully at ETFs: There are exchange traded funds based on an IPO index. As explained earlier in this book, ETFs have their own unique set of benefits and dangers. Remember, if the prevailing quality of IPOs is feeble, the quality of ETFs will also be weak. ETFs are designed to mirror the market they represent. The IPO universe is a fast-moving, high-risk game, and ETFs based on IPOs will reflect that.

The Google IPO

Just about the time we are convinced IPO investing is a miserable idea, an exception comes along, breaking all the rules and surprising everyone. In the prospectus for their offering, Google founders Larry Page and Sergey Brin confidently declared that their company would be different from others and that turned out to be true.

When Google went public in 2004 it had been in business for less than six years. Even so, Brin and Page had delayed the IPO as long as they were able. The time came when they could no longer avoid it. Their venture capitalists and private investors pushed for an IPO in order to get the expected return on their investment. And Google itself could use the cash an IPO would raise to enable its growth.

From the outset Google had an advantage over other high-tech start-ups that tried floating themselves on the stock market. Unlike some of its counterparts, Google had been up and running for a few years and it quickly achieved profitability, although its founders had managed to keep the company's dazzling profits from Internet search-targeted advertising a secret.

In the run-up to the public offering, financial experts estimated that Google would be valued at $30 billion. On April 29, 2004, Google filed its S-1, one of the requisite SEC pre-IPO documents.

The dot-com bubble had burst only a few years earlier and Silicon Valley IPOs were seen as tainted goods, yet Google's registration statement turned heads so fast that the investment world had whiplash. When analysts became aware of Google's strong advertising revenues and profit margins they thought this might be the next big deal.

Google revealed that it had generated 2003 revenues of $961.9 million with a net profit of $106.5 million. Sales rose 177 percent between 2002 and 2004. Google had been profitable since 2001 and was sitting on a bulging vault of $454.9 million in cash and cash equivalents.

Nevertheless, Larry Page alarmed prospective shareholders when he wrote, "Google is not a conventional company. We do not intend to become one. Throughout Google's evolution as a privately held company, we have managed Google differently. We have also emphasized an atmosphere of creativity and challenge, which has helped us provide unbiased, accurate and free access to information for those who rely on us around the world."[1]

To show their independence from Wall Street, the Google guys said they would not be providing earnings forecasts or guidance to industry analysts and declared they would make all decisions for the long-term good of the company. Most surprising of all, Google would forgo the traditional underwriting process and sell its IPO through an Internet-based Dutch auction. And to ensure that they could make good on the promise to be different, Google would have a double-tiered ownership structure that gave Page, Brin, and CEO Eric Schmidt total control over the company.

Google's initial public offering took place on August 18, 2004, with 19,605,052 shares selling at an opening price of $85 per share. Google's offering raised $1.67 billion, giving the company a market capitalization of $23 billion, somewhat short of expectations but still rich. To be sure, some money was left on the table, but a number of Google employees with shares in the company became overnight millionaires, and Page and Brin found themselves multibillionaires at age twenty-seven. Google was an instant favorite with individual investors and the stock price took off, once reaching a high of $715. Even though Google suffered in the severe market correction of 2007–8, it never declined to its IPO price.[2] In mid-2010 it was trading at around $500 per share.

Mergers and Acquisitions

Value investors often find themselves unintentionally at play in the mergers and acquisitions field. By the very nature of value guidelines they frequently buy the same undervalued companies that make attractive takeover targets. Value investors often purchase shares in companies in the mid- to small-capitalization range, since these companies are easier to evaluate and have fewer institutional holders. While some investors buy low-priced second- or third-tier companies in the specific hope that they will be acquired, this introduces more chance into the equation. Nevertheless, even Graham approved of this sort of speculation as long as it was intelligent, thought out, and well measured.

Like IPOs, mergers and acquisitions tend to proliferate at a certain phase in the business cycle. In the midst of a bear market, even if the market has bottomed only in a single industry, larger companies tend to gobble up their smaller, less entrenched competitors. In almost every recession the same pattern emerges.

The recession that began in 2007 was somewhat, although not entirely different. Because of the government bailout program, no doubt there were fewer M&As than might be expected. Government action provided protection for such organizations as AIG, Goldman Sachs, Fannie Mae, and Freddie Mac. M&A activity declined in 2009 when there were 28 percent fewer acquisitions than the year before.[3] This is consistent with the fact that share prices rebounded in 2009; the 19 percent market gain was the best in six years. Yet even with the bailout packages, there was some consolidation.

In 2009, for example, Pfizer, Merck & Company, and Bristol-Myers Squibb all made multibillion-dollar acquisition bids for smaller competitors. ExxonMobil acquired XTO Energy, and Oracle, which often grows by acquisition, purchased Sun Microsystems.

Reflection of the Trend Toward Globalization

M&A trends in the past thirty years have reflected the changing nature of the world economies. Business activity became increasingly global. Merger activity mimicked that trend exactly. In 1997 alone there were more than 2,333 cross-border transactions worth approximately $298 billion.

The 2009 $52 billion purchase of Anheuser-Busch by the Belgian company InBev was typical of this global trend. The combined company, Anheuser-Busch InBev, became the world's largest brewer with operations in more than 30 countries and sales in more than 130 countries. The brewer produces Budweiser, Michelob, Stella Artois, Bass, and other beers. Its nearest competitor is similarly global, London-based SABMiller.

Some of these transnational deals, including the merger of Germany's Daimler-Benz and the United States' Chrysler, brought dismal results. Nevertheless, they seemed strong at first glance and understanding them was a challenge for investors. When considering a position in a merger of equals or an acquisition situation, there are several points to consider:

- Asset valuation is similar to evaluating a company when purchasing shares. Look at historical earnings, future maintainable earnings, relative valuation, and discounted cash flow (DCF) valuations. It is also useful to compare similar companies and similar transactions.

- Most M&As do not produce the intended results, and it's usually more lucrative to be invested in the acquired company rather than the acquirer.

Most investors focus only on the profitability of the merged entity. Merger arbitrageurs, on the other hand, care only about the probability of the deal being completed or scrapped and about how long it will take the deal to close.

Kraft Foods

Kraft Foods' 2010 takeover of Britain's Cadbury PLC began on a seemingly friendly note with a tender offer from Kraft CEO Irene Rosenfeld. She may have known from day one that Cadbury management would bristle, and bristle they did. What followed was drama. Rosenfeld crossed the Atlantic to talk with Cadbury's board of directors, who accused her of behaving in an un-British way. Buffett, whose Berkshire Hathaway owns 9 percent of Kraft, also weighed in, insisting that Kraft was offering too much for Cadbury.

Still, the deal seemed sound. Both companies had sound financials and both owned leading food, snack, and confectionary products.

Kraft is the largest U.S. food company and the second largest in the world. It markets dozens of well-known snacks such as Oreo cookies and easily prepared foods such as macaroni and cheese in 155 countries. Kraft became a public company in 2001 and in 2008 became a component of the Dow Jones Industrial Average. It is a big company with more than $42 billion in revenues and 2009 net income of $2.9 billion.

Cadbury is an iconic chocolate candy brand around the world, and it also owns Dairy Milk chocolate, Hall's cough drops, Dentyne and Trident gums, and other brands.

Kraft offered Cadbury a combination of cash and its own shares for a total price of $17 billion. Cadbury said no, and Kraft quickly sold its North American pizza business to Nestlé for $3.7 billion to raise more cash for the Cadbury acquisition. Kraft upped its offer to $19.4 billion and the deal went through.

Wall Street did not warm to the Kraft-Cadbury merger, although Bill Ackman, manager of Pershing Square Capital, was the exception.

Several aspects made Kraft an interesting M&A play. Cadbury investors became part of a global market leader with a proven track record. Kraft shareholders acquired additional top-selling brands and would benefit from Cadbury's innovative investment in emerging markets. Ackman predicted that with Kraft's dividend and strong earnings of the combined organization, the shares would return 50 to 60 percent within two years of the merger. By mid-2010 Kraft's shares were up 15 percent from the time of acquisition

"I hesitate to call any acquisition a steal," said Ackman, "but this deal should ultimately prove to have been done at a very favorable price."[4]

Merger arbitrage, also called risk arbitrage, usually occurs when the merger is financed by a stock swap. The arbitrageur purchases the stock of the target company while short-selling the stock of the acquiring company.

Generally the market price of the target company is lower than the price offered by the acquiring company. The spread between these two prices depends mainly on the probability and the timing of the takeover being completed, as well as on the terms of the deal. After the merger is completed, the target's stock will be converted into stock of the acquirer based on the exchange ratio determined by the merger agreement. The arbitrageur delivers the necessary amount of converted stock into his short position to complete the arbitrage.

If this strategy represented easy money, many investors would adopt it, and gains for the arbitrageur would disappear. However, there are many unknowns. A major risk arises from the possibility of the merger failing to go through or the acquisition price being adjusted in a disadvantageous way. Obstacles may include either party's inability to satisfy conditions of the merger, a failure to obtain the requisite shareholder approval, failure to receive antitrust and other regulatory clearances, or some other event that may change the target's or the acquirer's willingness to consummate the transaction.

Preferred Stocks

Preferred shares are a hybrid between common stock and a bond. Those investing for income often favor preferreds because they normally pay a guaranteed dividend, which receives first priority over common stock dividends. Additionally, preferred stock shareholders step up before common stockholders when dividing up the company's assets in the event of bankruptcy. This gives preferred stocks an added element of safety, although they still remain subordinate to bondholders.

The terms of preferred stock issues can vary enormously. Perhaps the most important characteristic of a preferred stock is whether it is cumulative or noncumulative. In a cumulative issue, dividends that are in arrears build up. Before any dividend can be paid on the common stock, the entire unpaid balance must be paid to preferred holders. If a preferred issue is noncumulative and a dividend payment is missed, the shareholders are out of luck; they will probably never receive the missed dividends even if and when the company returns to prosperous times.

There are an endless number of other provisions that can affect the value of a preferred stock, including:

- Voting rights (or lack thereof)

- Whether the dividend rate is set, adjustable, or has a "participating factor" allowing an additional dividend if the company achieves a high net income

- Whether or not the preferred shares are convertible into common stock (more about that below)

Preferred shareholders forgo the possibility of capital gains in exchange for higher dividends and perceived safety, unless of course the shares are convertible.

There is an old Wall Street maxim, "Never convert a convertible stock," meaning that if you bought the stock for income and safety, you're usually best off sticking with that strategy.

In truth, preferred stocks probably don't make much sense for individual investors; however, they can be a lucrative investment for corporate portfolios. This is because individual investors must pay federal tax on the full dividend received, but corporations were only required to pay income tax on 30 percent of their preferred dividends. A full 70 percent of the income is tax free. Depending on interest rates and tax status, individual investors will probably receive a higher after-tax yield by investing in corporate bonds or municipal bonds. Additionally, corporate bonds usually have a senior claim over preferreds on assets in case of liquidation.

A word of caution to global investors: Regulations for preferred stocks vary from nation to nation. In certain countries, such as Canada and Great Britain, preferred shares are more commonly used and represent a much larger share of the stock market.

To learn more about which preferred shares are available, click on Income Investing Information at quantumonline.com. The site is free but will ask for a voluntary donation and will request that you register. Another way to invest in preferred stock is by buying a basket of them through an exchange traded fund. The S&P U.S. Preferred Stock Index fund (PFF) holds the preferred stocks for the S&P Index.

Convertibles

Convertible stocks and warrants are two different beasts, but they have one thing in common: their worth depends on the company's share price at some future date.

There is a tendency for companies to use more convertible securities in times of stress. Professional investors often prefer convertibles to common stocks in a high-risk atmosphere because it gives them greater flexibility.

When companies issue convertible securities, they do so to raise capital. Those that are unable to tap conventional sources of funding, usually because of low credit ratings, sometimes offer convertibles as a way to find cash and find it faster. When a corporation's reputation or credit has been sullied, it must pay a premium for new money, and this is how the opportunity, and the higher level of risk, come into play.

Convertibles frequently are bonds or preferred stocks that can be changed into something else—usually shares of the company's common stock. In certain cases, the holder of the convertible determines whether and when a conversion occurs. In other scenarios, the company retains the right to determine the terms of conversion.

In conventional convertible security financing, the conversion formula is fixed—meaning that the security converts into common stock based on a fixed price. The financing arrangements might also include caps on the price at which conversion may take place or other provisions to limit dilution—the reduction in earnings per share and proportional ownership that occurs when holders of convertible securities transfer those securities into common stock.

However, there are many variations on the conversion arrangement, and major investors, such as Buffett, often negotiate their own highly favorable terms. The convertibles he arranges are not available to the general public.

One of the downsides of convertible securities is that they will likely diminish the value of the common stock. The more convertibles sold and the lower the convertible price, the likelier this is to happen. The dilution can trigger a crisis: The greater the dilution, the greater the potential that the stock price per share will fall. The more the stock price falls, the harder it is for the company to obtain alternate financing and the greater the number of convertible shares it may need to offer in the future.

The SEC warns investors to take a close look at the details of the deal before buying a convertible stock. Find out what types of financings the company has engaged in and be sure to understand the effects those financings might have on the company and the value of all of its securities. This information can be found in the SEC's EDGAR database and by looking at the company's registration statements, annual and quarterly reports, and any interim reports that announce the transaction.

Warrants

A warrant is a security entitling the holder to buy stock of the issuing company at a specified price and date, which is typically higher than the price at time of issue, but less than investors believe the shares could trade at in the future. Warrants are another way for a company to borrow money and often are attached to bonds or preferred stock as a sweetener, allowing the issuer to pay lower interest rates or dividends. They are used to enhance the yield of a security and make it more attractive to potential buyers.

As a type of option, a warrant has an exercise price and an expiration date. The exercise price is the price at which the holder may convert the warrant into common shares of the issuer. The expiration date is the last date on which the warrant can be converted into common shares. The expiration date is usually two or more years from issuance. This allows warrants to trade separately from the bond with which they were issued.

Frequently, these warrants are detachable, and can be sold independently of the bond or stock. Warrants are actively traded in some financial markets such as Deutsche Börse and the Hong Kong exchange.

Benjamin Graham often warned that warrants could be used in a manipulative way and that investors should pay nothing extra for them. That way, if down the road the warrants can be sold at a premium, they truly were a sweetener for the deal.

When considering the value of warrants, these are the desirable factors:

- A low price

- A long duration

- An option or purchase price near the current market price

Bankruptcy Plays

The years between 2007 and 2009 were earthquake years for corporate collapse. The 2008 $691 million Lehman Brothers Holdings failure was the largest bankruptcy in U.S. history. Chrysler Corporation's Chapter 11 reorganization was another blow to the American psyche. The collapse of IndyMac Bancorp and American Home Mortgage Investment Corporation brought agony to millions of investors and home owners. Many of America's favorite old companies such as the Sun-Times Media Group, Ritz Camera Centers, and Lillian Vernon went away.

Clearly there would have been more and larger bankruptcies without the government bailout of companies considered "too big to fail." The controversial Troubled Asset Relief Program (TARP) began in October 2008 under President George W. Bush and continued through the first year of President Barack Obama's presidency. TARP included the purchase of $40 billion of preferred stock in AIG, $25 billion of preferred stock in Citigroup, and $15 billion of preferred stock in Bank of America, and it also guaranteed a $306 billion portfolio of assets owned by Citigroup. Additionally the U.S. Treasury lent billions of dollars to General Motors and Chrysler.

Two different questions arise for investors when a company goes into bankruptcy. First, if you are already in the stock, should you get out? The second question is whether or not the bankruptcy presents a unique investment opportunity.

The answers depend on a variety of factors, the foremost being whether the company has entered Chapter 7 or Chapter 11 bankruptcy proceedings.

If it is a Chapter 7 filing, then the questions become moot. The business is over. The company will be liquidated, and if you were holding shares you will get money back only if there is anything remaining after all creditors are paid. It's now out of your hands.

If the company has entered into Chapter 11 proceedings, or reorganization, the shares can continue to trade. Even though the company may no longer qualify for listing on a major exchange, it could be bought and sold privately, through the Pink Sheets or through other channels. No longer in printed format, Pink Sheets is a real-time electronic system reporting market maker information for over-the-counter stocks.

Chapter 11 bankruptcy allows the company to restructure under court protection and supervision. This becomes a "work out," or a situation that relies on court and management action rather than economic issues. Large, well-financed investors such as Warren Buffett sometimes participate profitably in work-out situations because they can lend money to finance a recovery, demanding terms that smaller organizations or individual investors could never achieve.

It is difficult to determine the value of shares of a company in bankruptcy. The company's normal book value gets shredded. Intangibles such as goodwill and relationships with existing customers are damaged, sometimes beyond repair. To right their situation, officers usually begin selling tangible assets. However, because those acquiring the assets know the seller is in distress, they usually are able to pay less than their true worth.

Writing for the Motley Fool, Bill Mann says, "So, potential speculators, bottom dwellers, and Dumpster divers, the answer is that as a rule, investing in bankrupt companies (or even soon-to-be bankrupt companies) is a horrible idea. I'm in fact baffled that the SEC and the exchanges even allow companies in Chapter 11 to trade at all—the implied return on the vast majority of these companies is exactly zero."[5]

Mann continued, "Look at it this way: Would you rather have more than 20,000 shares of Lehman [Brothers Holdings] for $4,000 or one share of Berkshire Hathaway (NYSE: BRK-B) for the same amount? The chance of Berkshire going to zero is next to nil; the chance of Lehman being anything but zero is just as remote. In the end, $4,000 is $4,000."[6]

Bankruptcies are all very sad and disturbing, but there are lessons to be learned.

■ When a company is headed for bankruptcy, share price can dissolve like an Airborne tablet dropped into a glass of water. It fizzles away. On September 15, 2008, it seemed that AIG was heading for bankruptcy; the next day, September 16, 2008, AIG's stock dropped 60 percent. When holding stocks with the potential for bankruptcy, investors should protect themselves in some way. As explained earlier, hedging is a traditional strategy, but unless it is a large holding at high risk, the cost of hedging may cut into potential profits so deeply that most individual investors don't do it. The easiest strategy is to sell your shares as soon as you understand the extent of the trouble, thereby avoiding additional stress. You may also place a stop loss order to sell at a price below which you no longer wish to hold the shares. The difference between trading price and the sell order should be wide enough so that the stock is not sold due to normal market gyrations.

- When there is a bankruptcy, it sometimes means an entire industry is under stress. In the case of newspapers, it is clear that the industry will never be the same and investors should adjust their thinking. But since most people want to know what's happening in the world and information is vital to the workings of democracy, free enterprise, and most of the world's activities, ask the questions: What will replace traditional news sources? Is there an investment opportunity there? Such reasoning may have led you to an investment in Google Inc. or perhaps even a radio broadcasting stock such as Clear Channel Communications.

- In vital industries not likely to go away, such as food and energy production, medical services, banking, and automobiles, there will always be survivors. If a company goes bankrupt and is unlikely to recover, look to its competitors to determine who will grab the dying company's market share. Even though Ford Motor Company has struggled for years, many investors were drawn to it after GM and Chrysler got into trouble. Ford, they believed, had a solid plan going forward and would be saddled with less debt than its competitors. True, this is vulture investing, but it is the way capitalism works and it keeps the economy in constant adjustment, so don't feel guilty.

Chapter 12

Looking to Do Better

*If you were to put your money away and not look at it for many years,
until you were ready for retirement, when you finally looked at it, you'd
probably faint with amazement at how much money is there.*[1]

JOHN BOGLE

W e often hear stories of people like Grace Groner, who made a simple investment, stuck with it, and dazzled the world with what she accomplished. Groner was orphaned during the Great Depression; she never married and never held a high-paying job. A family in her town raised her and sent her to Lake Forest College in Illinois. She then went to work for Abbott Laboratories as a secretary, a job she held for forty-three years.[2]

In 1935 Grace purchased three $60 shares of specially issued Abbott stock and held on to them. The stock split many times over the next seventy-five years, and Groner reinvested all dividends. When she died in 2010 at age one hundred, Groner left her money to Lake Forest College. To everyone's surprise, her $180 was by then worth $7 million. Compounded at the typical rate of inflation, 3 percent, over that time period she would have only had a little over $67,000. She also left her tiny one-bedroom home to the college. It became a residence for women on scholarships and would be called Grace's Cottage.

Imagine how the markets heaved and billowed during those seventy-five years. Imagine how often investors were told to diversify.

Grace may have been advised to buy some gold, look to global markets, and do lots of clever things. But she just went on with her simple, conservative approach. It probably wasn't even a strategy. She just kept it going and it worked.

Why am I telling you this story now, after warning that a buy-and-hold strategy is chancy in these markets and presenting all the ideas, techniques, and strategies we've discussed throughout this book?

There are two reasons.

First, Grace Groner's story puts investing into long-term focus. Some predictions for the U.S. and even global markets indicate we're going into a deep economic winter that could last at least for another decade.[3] While a smart person is always prepared for the worst, he also should seek the best outcome. Negative predictions can become a self-filling prophecy. Groner bought her initial stock at the darkest hour of the Great Depression. From that time until her death there were thirteen recessions of various magnitudes. But she kept plugging away, and ended up $7 million to the good.

Second, this is a book of rules—rules for sane investing, especially in times of trouble.

Ben Graham often said there are no sure and easy paths to riches on Wall Street, and quite often the simplest road is the best of all the roads available to travel. He admonished investors to have the right attitude, use common sense, and think for themselves. Surely Graham would agree that Grace Groner did just that.

Rule #1: Maintain the Right Attitude

The first objective of the value investor is to protect your principal, to not lose money. Simple logic will show you that it is better to trade safety for a somewhat lower return, while at the same time keeping the cost of investing down. If your portfolio earns a little less than that of the guy in the next cubicle over, don't let resentment take hold in your mind. He may be pushing the risk. If you still have your primary investment and it earns out at a reasonable rate, you will continue to grow and compound your assets. If you lose your savings or investment, you have nothing to build on. A zero investment account earns zero returns.

Rule #2: Ignore Predictions and Projections

Everyone seems to have an opinion on the economy and a whole lot of people offer tips for hot stocks. Hooting and hollering about the stock market goes on at earsplitting decibels. Oddly, when the market is rising higher, the prognosticators often agree that it will keep climbing; when the market is on its back, their outlook tends to think it will stay that way indefinitely.

"I have no use whatsoever for projections or forecasts," says Buffett. "They create an illusion of apparent precision. The more meticulous they are, the more concerned you should be. We never look at projections but we care very much about and look very deeply at track records. If a company has a lousy track record but a very bright future, we will miss the opportunity."[4]

Charlie Munger insists that projections usually do more harm than good, especially those promoted aggressively by investment firm analysts and the media. "They are put together by people who have an interest in a particular outcome, have a subconscious bias, and its apparent precision makes it fallacious. They remind me of Mark Twain's saying, 'a mine is a hole in the ground owned by a liar.' Projections in America are often a lie although not an intentional one, but the worst kind because the forecaster often believes them himself."[5]

Those strong opinions do not mean that you should not look at a potential investment from all angles. Investing and building a stock portfolio depend on thinking about both past and future performance, but even Graham, with all his scholarship, warned that projections of future performance could only be a "rough index" to what lies ahead. Work into your calculations a little leeway for errors—that important margin of safety—and sleep well at night, he said.

Rule #3: Stick to the Facts

William O'Neil tells us time and again that mere opinion isn't enough reason to buy or sell. "A trap people get into is using personal opinion. Personal opinion can easily be wrong." While strong, entrenched opinions can skew our view of reality, Buffett and other master investors show us that intuition, when it is based on training, experience, and information, is a powerful investment tool. However, that intuition must evolve from knowledge and sound judgment.

Rule #4: Watch for Those Marching Out of Step

David Iben points out that when everyone starts doing the same thing, they usually do it to excess. "I will point out that whenever one industry becomes 30 percent of [any] index, such as technology was in 1999 and finance was in 1997, it means it is popular. It also means a lot of capital goes into one area and that will create excess supply and hurt margins. When everyone is in one area, it's good to be somewhere else."

Often these out-of-step companies he favors are solid businesses with a competitive advantage and a healthy profit margin.

Contrarians make a practice of looking for a superior company that nobody loves, such as Kraft Foods. The market often is out of alignment with the true value of these background companies, sometimes sending the price above and other times tumbling it below intrinsic value.

At a time when the economy was in the depths of despair, John Deere, manufacturer of tractors and other farm equipment, beat all analysts' expectations for 2009 net income. Unexpectedly the company's stock rose 5 percent during the same time the S&P 500 was down 0.3 percent.[6]

Rule #5: Steer Clear of Leverage

"Just about the only way a smart person can go broke is to borrow money," says Buffett. "While there's nothing more fun than leverage on the way up, there is nothing more deadly than leverage on the way down. If you're smart you don't need it and you shouldn't use it. Using borrowed money was rampant [as the markets were rising]. If enough other people are doing foolish things you have to be extra careful that foolish things don't destroy you."

Maneuver in the direction of companies with little or no debt, lots of free cash flow, and wisely deployed capital.

Additionally, says Buffett, don't think of your own home as an investment or as a source of cash to buy a boat, invest in more real estate, or start new businesses. "The present housing debacle should teach home buyers, lenders, brokers and government some simple lessons that will ensure stability in the future. Home purchases should involve an honest-to-God down payment of at least 10 percent and monthly payments that can be comfortably handled by the borrower's income. That income should be carefully verified."[7]

Rule #6: Embrace Volatility

Much of the time stock market volatility is nothing more than short-term noise.

David Iben of Nuveen's Tradewinds Global Investors says this condition has not changed since Graham's day. "We all know that the market is cyclical at best, alternating between bipolar inflated and depressed prices relative to the value of the underlying business."[8]

"I love aberrant markets," Iben continues. "It is exciting when markets start behaving contrary to how the fundamentals suggest they ought to. Think small cap stocks in 1999, junk bonds in 1991, or large cap stocks and long bonds in 1982. The anomalies created the closest thing to 'free money' that I've witnessed in my career."[9]

He's not the only one who feels this way. Charles Brandes saw the positive side of the 2007–8 market implosion. "We know that past performance does not guarantee future results, but we think history can be instructive," says Brandes. "We think that when people look back on this period they will consider this one of the most timely and rewarding periods to invest."[10] Brandes went on to explain that historically and logically, when the market is in crisis and prices are at a low level, bargains may be scattered in the street waiting to be gathered up.

Rule #7: Listen to the Sailor Within

While it is true that value investors do not fear volatility and do not try to time the investment markets, many of the tools used in this book are weather vanes. They provide warning signs that stormy seas are ahead. Sometimes it takes many months of overheated markets before the cooldown comes, but it does come. As gravity would explain, the trip down is often faster than the trip up. All investors, even those in ETFs and mutual funds, should keep an eye on what the market is up to and should adjust their investment course as necessary.

There are several sayings involving watercraft that apply quite well to investors. For example, "A rising tide lifts all boats." Conversely, a receding tide also strands all those boats that don't head out to safer water. And then there is this one: The sailor tacks into the wind to move forward. If the wind comes from one direction to another, he adjusts his sails. When the wind shifts, he adjusts again. No matter which way the wind is blowing, he can still head for his chosen port. There are two dangerous winds—one that is blowing the market into overvalues, and the other that is blowing your individual stock into high waters. So we build strong boats, captain them skillfully, but when we know a big storm is forecast, we set sail for a safe harbor.

Warren Buffett did this in 1969 when the stock market was overblown. He told his clients that he simply couldn't find solid, well-priced stocks to buy, and he closed down his partnership.

Rule #8: Step Back from a Smoking Hot Market

Seth Klarman says investors must always expect the unexpected and take precautions in advance of any sudden turn of events. They should be loaded for bear, even when there is no bear in sight. Generally, the best strategy is to buy stocks, not the stock market. Decisions are made on the basis of the fundamentals of the shares you own. That strategy, plus the ability to recognize an overheated stock market, puts your portfolio in a safe zone. Watch for these signs of generalized overvalue:

- Price levels are at historic heights.

- Price-to-earnings ratios skyrocket.

- Dividend yields are unpopular, low historically, and low compared with bond market yields.

- There is a rash of new stock offerings.

- Margin buying is on the rise.

- The stock indexes become increasingly volatile.

It seems that investors keep repeating mistakes of the past when it comes to overexuberance in the stock market. "Well, these are age old lessons," mused Buffett. "There aren't new lessons. These are the things we all knew that many people forget when they're euphoric."

Rule #9: Diversify

If we all had perfect judgment and foresight, there would be no need to diversify. If all asset classes rose and fell in tandem, it wouldn't be necessary to spread risk. Diversity builds a broad financial base for strength and stability.

"Additionally, I'll say it again—everyone should own some gold," repeats David Iben. "Real estate, stocks and hard assets also deserve a space in everyone's portfolio. Real estate should be focused on the nonbubble markets of the world and stock portfolios ought to be diversified globally."[11]

Rule #10: Inflation Happens—Be Ready for It

Inflation is the invisible, insidious enemy. It has destroyed many economies, hurt companies, and diminished the well-being of many individuals.

"Inflation is going to affect you," says Buffett. "Long term, even a small amount is bad." He says the very best defense against inflation is a person's own earning power. "The second best is owning a wonderful business, such as Coke, that doesn't require capital. With Coke, you'll get your share of national earnings."[12]

Rule #11: Accept a Few Mistakes

Know you are going to make some investment errors, prepare for them, forgive yourself, and move on. Buffett wrote in his 2009 letter to shareholders that he'd erred in buying a chunk of ConocoPhillips. "I in no way anticipated the dramatic fall in energy prices that occurred in the last half of the year." He was up front about admitting the scale of his mistake: "The terrible timing of my purchase has cost Berkshire several billion dollars." Over the years Buffett has admitted to many mistakes. He sometimes jokes that he had to enroll in AA (Airlines Anonymous) to kick the habit of investing in airlines. But his superior choices have more than counterbalanced his poor ones, and Berkshire Hathaway keeps piling in the cash.

Rule #12: Have a Good Time

Investing should be fun, challenging, and deeply satisfying. Think of investing as a great adventure in a fascinating world.

A Simple Checklist

Seek out companies with a good track record and an honest, ethical, and smart management team. Based on your findings, structure a low-cost, low-maintenance portfolio built for the greatest strength and survivability:

- Create a portfolio of approximately thirty equities using the guidelines below.

- Set a target. For example, if an individual stock does not appreciate 50 percent above cost within two years, replace it with a better choice.

When buying stocks, insist on:

- An attractive price-to-earnings ratio based on the discussion in chapters 6 and 9.

- A price near or below book value.

- A price well below the previous high, perhaps one half the market high of the past two years.

- An appealing price in relation to past earnings growth. For example, a P/E lower than the company's own seven- to ten-year average.

- A suitable dividend yield, if dividends are what you need. Remember, total return is the combination of dividend yield and share price appreciation, so the dividend is never to be discounted as unimportant.

Lessons We Should Have Learned as a Nation

"The lessons of the Bubble Decade are still being formed," wrote Neil Irwin in *The Washington Post.* "At the Federal Reserve, the major lesson that top officials have taken is that bank regulation shouldn't occur in a vacuum; rather than monitor how individual institutions are doing, bank supervisors should try to understand the risks and frailties that the banking system creates for the economy as a whole—and manage those risks."[13]

The questions on Wall Street and in Washington now are how to prevent a recurrence of the zero-growth decade and how to return to a thriving economy.

"One of our challenges now," President Obama said, "is how do we get what I call a postbubble growth model, one that is sustainable."[14]

Seth Klarman observed that the "near-death experience" of the previous few years should have taught Wall Street something. "Yet one year after the 2008 collapse, investors have returned to shockingly speculative behavior."[15]

There are tremendous advantages to capitalism and free markets, and the innovation, experimentation, and rational risk taking that characterize capitalism must be cultivated. But as old philosophy professors like to say, "Your freedom to swing your fist ends where my nose begins." When business and financial activities take advantage of or mislead, gamble with other people's money, and unfairly damage investors, that's where the restraints should be.

The tricky part is the balancing act. A major point of education from the crisis of 2007–8 is that self-regulation alone does not work. We need stronger regulation and surveillance of banking and especially of the creation and marketing of derivatives and other new, complex financial products.

"There were a lot of crazy things going on because people got rewarded for short-term behavior," says Charles Brandes. "We will also see a lot of destruction by people who were overpaid. Some people lost jobs, some lost their investments, some were totally wiped out."

In the summer of 2010 Congress passed the Wall Street and Consumer Protection Act in an effort to curb some of the past abuses. The bill included banking and derivative trading reform, executive pay, and other matters.

Greek prime minister George Papandreou says that while many people fear the word "regulation" because it appears to slow progress, regulations are also necessary. He used a simple analogy: traffic lights that help establish order and predictability on roads. "People might say, we don't need traffic lights because they slow down cars. They do slow down cars but they prevent accidents. They do help us."[16]

When Papandreou was elected in October 2009 he discovered that the previous administration had grossly understated the national debt. At $410 billion, it was four times the amount that citizens of Greece had been told. The public debt represented 12.7 percent of the gross domestic product. Shockingly, it appeared that several U.S. financial firms had helped the former Greek government structure deals with derivatives and other products that masked the enormity of the debt. Additionally, some of the same investment houses used credit default swaps to literally bet that Greece would not be able to pay off the loans they had arranged. This is like a boxer secretly betting that he will lose a fight. U.S. Senate Banking Committee chairman Christopher Dodd said that the deals by "major financial firms are amplifying a public crisis for what would appear to be for private gain."[17]

Bear markets come, recessions fall upon us, and even sound stocks can go awry in prosperous years. But by wit and wisdom, people work through these difficulties to better times. So keep your chin up and look for the best places to put your money now. At the May 2009 Berkshire Hathaway annual meeting, Buffett admitted to being caught doing a few "dumb things in investments." But he professed his optimism for investing over the long term. "Our country has faced far worse travails in the past," he said, but invariably, "we've overcome them."

"America's best days lie ahead," he said. To prove his point, that year Berkshire Hathaway experienced one of its best performances ever with a net worth gain of $21.8 billion, or 19.8 percent. If you had invested $10,000 with Buffett when he began building Berkshire Hathaway on October 1, 1964, equivalent to $60,000 today, your investment would now be worth about $80 million.

ACKNOWLEDGMENTS

I would like to express my appreciation to the following people from Portfolio / Penguin for their valuable contributions: Alissa Amell, Emily Angell, Matthew Boezi, Laura M. Clark, Courtney Young, and Adrian Zackheim. Also, thanks to Alan Bradford, Charles Brandes, Warren Buffett, David Iben, and William O'Neil for time they spent sharing their expert opinions. My literary representative, Alice F. Martell, did a fine job, as always.

Acid test ratio—See Quick ratio.

American depositary receipt (ADR)—A way U.S. citizens can buy and sell publicly traded foreign-based companies. The receipt shows that shares of an overseas corporation are held on deposit or under the control of a U.S. bank. The bank acts as a transfer agent and collects any dividends on behalf of the holder.

Asset allocation—The distribution of investment funds among various categories of securities, such as bonds, stocks, global investments, utility companies, high technology, or the like. Studies imply that if investors can anticipate the best category in which to invest, returns can be maximized.

Balance sheet—A financial statement demonstrating a company's assets, liabilities, and capital at a specific time.

Bear market—Typically a bear turns and runs away when confronted (although, sadly, not always). In a bear market, stock prices are in retreat, or declining over a substantial number of weeks or months.

Beta—The beta of a stock or portfolio is a number describing the relation of its returns with that of the financial market as a whole. An asset with a beta of 0 indicates that its price is *not* correlated with the market. In other words, the asset is independent. A positive beta shows that the asset generally follows the market. A negative beta means that the asset moves in the opposite direction to the market; the asset generally decreases in value if the market goes up and vice versa.

Book value—Total assets minus intangible assets minus liabilities minus stock issues ahead of common stock. To arrive at book value per share, follow the same steps, then divide by the number of shares outstanding. Book value of an issue such as preferred or secondary preferred stock is calculated by subtracting all issues that take precedence over it, then dividing by the number of shares outstanding.

Bull market—Bulls charge madly forward. A bull market is on a sustained rise in value.

Business cycle—Predictable patterns of sales and profits within specific industries. Often the share prices of companies within the industries rise and fall in tandem with the business cycle.

Call option—Commonly referred to as a call. A call gives the buyer a right to purchase a specific number of shares at a specific price by a fixed date. The call expires after that date. The opposite of a call is a put.

Capital gain (loss)—Profit or loss from the sale of a capital asset. Short-term capital gains are those realized in less than six months.

Capitalization—The total value of various securities issued by a corporation.

Cash—In accounting parlance, this category comprises cash, marketable securities, and any asset that may be used to temporarily park money.

Cash flow—A company's net income (after taxes), plus the amounts written off for depreciation, depletion, amortization, and other charges.

Common stock—A unit of ownership in a company. Owners of common stock receive dividends after owners of preferred stock. Their claim to assets is junior to all other types of stock in the event of liquidation.

Confirmation of Dow signals—When either the Dow Jones Industrial Average or Transportation Average moves into new high or low territory, the other average must do likewise for the movement to indicate a meaningful trend. Either average may penetrate first.

Contrarian—An investor who does the opposite of what most investors are doing. Contrarians believe that if everyone believes something will happen, it won't. This is because when people collectively believe in an event—that the DJIA is about to plunge, for example—they all take corrective action. This prevents the actual event from occurring. When investors believe a stock is a bargain because it is going to rise, they buy the stock, which drives the price up. Contrarians like to buy ignored stocks and wait for them to be discovered.

Credit default swap—A financial arrangement or swap designed to transfer the credit exposure of fixed income products between parties.

Current asset—Cash or something of value that can be converted into cash within a year.

Current liability—An obligation due for payment within one year.

Current ratio—Current assets divided by current liabilities. Though standards vary from one industry to the next, most analysts like companies to have a current ratio of 2 to 1, or twice as many current assets as current liabilities.

Day trading—The speculative practice of buying and selling financial instruments within the same trading day, closing out all positions before the market closes for the day. Trading can be done in stocks, stock options, currencies, and various futures contracts such as equity index futures, interest rate futures, and commodity futures. The practice is also called active trading.

Depression—A severe and sustained downturn in economic activity lasting several years.

Derivatives—Any financial instruments in which the return is linked to, or derived from, the performance of some underlying asset such as bonds or currencies or commodities. Futures and options are the most common forms of derivatives. The more exotic derivatives have catchy names such as inverse floater, swap, and cap and collar.

Dilution—A reduction in the percentage of ownership of the common stockholder by the issuance of additional common shares for less than the current market price.

Dividend—The distribution of the earnings of a company to shareholders. Dividend payments are not required except on certain classes of stock, and common stock dividends can vary in amount. The amount is determined each year by the board of directors. Most often dividends are paid in cash, but they can be paid in additional shares of stock, scrip, company products, or property.

Dividend rate—The amount of annual dividend per share.

Dividend yield—The ratio of dividend paid to the market price. A stock selling for $100 and paying a dividend of $5 has a dividend yield of 5 percent. Also sometimes called dividend ratio or dividend return.

Dollar cost averaging—Buying a specific dollar amount of a stock each month, regardless of price. This way an investor buys more shares when the price is low and fewer shares when the price is high. The buyer also pays a lower than average price for the shares, since he does not risk buying too many shares at too high of a price.

Double bottom—When a stock declines, reaches a cyclical low, rallies, and then declines again to at or near the earlier low price. If the second decline stops near, but not below, the first low point, Charles Dow believed that the subsequent rally could well be the beginning of a strong upward movement.

Double top—As a stock advances, the price may suddenly suffer a reversal. If it once again advances to its former high (or very near to it) and declines again, it is said to have seen a double top. Charles Dow felt that a decline from the second top is likely to be severe.

Dow Jones averages—Traditionally, three different market averages were computed by the Dow Jones company, the industrial, transportation, and utility averages. Today, Dow Jones offers many different averages, both domestic and global.

Earnings per share—A company's net income (after taxes) divided by the number of common shares outstanding.

Earnings rate—The amount of annual earnings per share, expressed in dollars.

Earnings yield—The ratio of annual earnings to market price. A stock earning $5 and selling at $50 has an earnings yield of 10 percent. Sometimes called the price-to-earnings ratio or yield.

EDGAR—Government-run Internet site providing information, reports, and documents for all registered, publicly traded companies in the United States.

Enterprise value—The value of a company as an ongoing business, or its economic worth to its owners.

Exchange traded fund (ETF)—An investment vehicle traded on stock exchanges much like stocks. An ETF is made up of assets such as stocks or bonds and trades at approximately the same price as the net asset value of its underlying securities. Most ETFs track an index, such as the S&P 500 or the Dow Jones Industrial Average. ETFs can be attractive as investments because of their low costs, diversification, and similarity to stocks. Put another way, ETFs are index funds that are traded in the financial markets.

Fixed assets—An accounting term referring to land, buildings, equipment, and furnishings.

Free cash flow yield—An overall return evaluation ratio of a stock, which standardizes the free cash flow per share a company is expected to earn against its market price per share. The ratio is calculated by taking the free cash flow per share divided by the share price.

Fundamental analysis—A philosophy whereby stocks are regarded as fractional ownership of the underlying business that they represent.

Goodwill—An accounting term referring to the difference between the value of assets and the price paid for them. It also refers to a value placed on a company's reputation, patents, trademarks, location, and other qualities that give a company competitive advantage.

Hedge fund—An investment company that is set up as a limited partnership and uses high-risk methods in quest of exceptional returns. These specialty funds are permitted by regulators to undertake a wider range of investment and trading activities than other investment funds. Generally, investment managers are paid a performance fee. Each hedge fund has its own investment strategy that determines the types of investments and the methods of investment it uses.

Federal legislation passed in 2010 placed tighter regulation and new disclosure requirements on hedge funds.

Income statement—Also called the earnings report or profit and loss (P&L) statement. It reflects revenues and expenses over an accounting period, usually one quarter or one year.

Index arbitrage—A form of program trading.

Initial public offering—The first sale of its shares by a private company to the public. An IPO is sometimes called a float. Smaller, newer companies seeking to raise capital often issue IPOs. They do this for several reasons, including the owners' wish for greater liquidity for their own capital. An IPO can also be floated by large privately owned companies looking to become publicly traded.

Intangibles—An accounting term referring to difficult-to-measure assets such as goodwill, brands and trademarks, leaseholds, and reputation. Though companies can easily overstate intangibles, they can also have enormous worth. The Coca-Cola brand name is an example of a highly valuable intangible.

Intrinsic value—The fundamental value of a company based on its ability to produce profits, or its true worth to its owners, as opposed to the company's share price or perceived value.

Junior security—Security with lower priority to claim a company's assets and income. Common stock is subordinate to debt issues and preferred stock, for example.

Leverage—The use of debt to increase purchasing power.

Liquidation value—The cash a company would gather if it sold all its assets and paid off all its debts.

Margin—Buying a security on credit.

Margin call—An order by a brokerage firm for the investor to pay off an outstanding loan. This could mean the investor has to sell the security that secures the loan.

Margin of safety—The concept that potential investments should be evaluated so as to leave a margin for error. Elements in the selection of a stock or bond or creation of a portfolio should be such as to protect against mistakes or unexpected developments, in much the same way that an engineer designs a bridge to bear a heavier weight than would ever be expected. There are various theories on how to achieve a margin of safety.

Modern portfolio theory—The concept that a risk-averse investor can construct a portfolio optimizing or maximizing expected return based on a given level of market risk, acknowledging that risk is an inherent part of higher reward. The idea is also called "portfolio theory" or "portfolio management theory." Harry Markowitz pioneered the theory.

Multiple—A synonym for the price-to-earnings ratio or P/E.

National debt—The national debt is the total amount of money owed by the government; the federal budget deficit is the yearly amount by which spending exceeds revenue. Add up all the yearly deficits (and subtract those few budget surpluses we've had) and you'll get the current national debt.

Net current asset value—The difference between current assets and current liabilities.

Net income—The income for a company after deducting all expenses.

Net-net—Assets *minus* current liabilities *minus* long-term debt.

Operating income—Corporate income after deducting expenses, except taxes, from normal operations.

Overtrading—Buying on a margin basis in larger amounts than is prudent considering the resources of the investor.

Paper profit (loss)—The unrealized amount above or below the purchase price of a security at which it could be currently sold. The profit or loss is still on paper because the investor in fact still owns the security.

Par value—An arbitrary price intended to indicate the initial price of a corporation's shares. This does not necessarily mean that the shares originally went to market at this price.

Portfolio—Total investment holdings of an individual or other entity.

Price-to-earnings ratio—A calculation showing how much must be paid for $1 of earnings. The P/E ratio is derived by dividing the share price by the company's previous twelve-month per-share earnings. For example, if the stock sells at $26 per share and the earnings are $2 per share, the P/E is 13 to 1. The P/E is sometimes called the multiple.

Primary movement (in the stock market)—A substantial upward swing in the market, which will be tempered by a movement in the opposite direction (see Secondary movement). Charles H. Dow felt that the magnitude of a primary movement was difficult, if not impossible, to predict in advance.

Profit and loss statement—Frequently called an income statement or P&L, this accounting document is a summary of a company's revenues and expenses during a specific period. Together with the balance sheet, this document depicts a company's full financial picture.

Program trading—The simultaneous trading of a portfolio of stocks, as opposed to buying or selling just one stock at a time. The New York Stock Exchange defines program trading as any trade involving fifteen or more stocks with an aggregate value in excess of $1 million. Typically, orders from the trader's computer are entered directly into the market's computer system and executed automatically. Index arbitrage is another form of program trading.

Prospectus—A document giving details about an offer to sell securities and/or mutual funds. The Securities and Exchange Commission ordinarily must approve the document for an initial public offering before it is circulated.

Proxy—A document authorizing one person (often company management) to vote the shares of another person (often the shareholder).

Pump and dump—One of the most common stock frauds, especially common on the Internet. A company will send out a glowing news release about its financial health or a new product or innovation. A newsletter purporting to offer unbiased recommendations quickly touts the company as the latest hot stock. The same idea is planted on message rooms and bulletin boards, urging investors to buy the stock while it's still affordable. Investors then buy the stock, driving the price higher as predicted. Insiders or fraudsters then quickly dump their stock at a profit. The price falls again, leaving unsuspecting investors with a loss.

Put—Technically called a put option, this contract gives a seller the right to sell a specific number of shares at a specific price by a certain date. The put option buyer pays the seller a premium for this right. For example, a purchaser of an ABC December 50 put has the right to sell 100 shares of ABC at $50 to the put seller at any time until the contract expires in December. The buyer expects the stock price to fall, while the seller expects the price to remain stable, rise, or drop by an amount less than his or her profit on the premium. This is the opposite of a call option.

Qualitative analysis—Analysis based on nonnumerical factors, such as market share, location of business, industry group, name recognition, or the like.

Quantitative analysis—Analysis based on financial statement numbers.

Quick ratio—Also known as "acid test ratio." An indicator of a company's short-term liquidity. The quick ratio measures a company's ability to meet its short-term obligations with its most liquid assets. The quick ratio is calculated by subtracting inventory from current assets, and dividing that number by current liabilities. The higher the quick ratio, the better the position of the company. The quick ratio is more conservative than the current ratio.

Recession—Most economists agree that an economic recession can only be confirmed after gross domestic product growth is negative for two or more consecutive quarters.

Red herring—A prospectus for an initial public offering of corporate shares. It is called a red herring because it contains warnings of risk throughout, printed in red.

Retained earnings—Corporate net income that has not been distributed to shareholders, but rather held in corporate coffers for specific or general use.

Return on invested capital—Net income plus interest expense divided by total capitalization.

Secondary movement (in the stock market)—According to Charles H. Dow, the law of action and reaction demands that a primary movement in the market will have a secondary movement in the opposite direction of at least three eighths of the primary movement. For example, if a stock advances 10 points, it is likely to relapse 4 points. Dow said the same rule applies to movements of individual stocks.

Securities and Exchange Commission (SEC)—A U.S. government agency that regulates and supervises the securities industry. It was established in the New Deal of the 1930s.

Securities and Exchange Commission (SEC) documents—The SEC requires certain documents to be filed by publicly traded corporations at specific times. Form 10-K is an annual business and financial report; Form 10-Q is the quarterly financial report; a Form 8-K must be filed within fifteen days of unscheduled material events or corporate changes. Additionally, companies must file proxy statements for annual meetings, merger proxy statements in the case of a merger, and a prospectus when new shares are to be offered to the public.

Senior security—A security that ranks above common stock in the event of liquidation, such as a bond or preferred stock.

Unless otherwise indicated, first-person accounts and quotes for this book from the following individuals are from interviews conducted by the author on the dates listed below:

Charles Brandes, October 12 and 13, 2009.

Warren Buffett, October 14, 2009.

David Iben, November 11, 2009.

William O'Neil, December 7, 2009.

Chapter 1: Value Investing in Troubled Times

1. Jason Zweig, "If You Think the Worst Is Over, Take Benjamin Graham's Advice," *The Wall Street Journal*, May 26, 2009.

2. Daniel Myers, "Benjamin Graham: Three Timeless Principles," Forbes .com, February 23, 2009.

3. "The Stock Market Is Like a Pendulum," *Forbes*, June 15, 1975, p. 36.

Chapter 2: Value Investing in the Twenty-first Century

1. John C. Bogle, *The Little Book of Common Sense Investing* (Hoboken, NJ: John Wiley & Sons), 2007, p. xi.

2. Michael Brush, MSN Money, MSN.com, November 5, 2009.

3. www.Investopedia.com.

4. Berkshire Hathaway 1994 annual report, p. 5. Copyrighted material reproduced with the permission of Warren Buffett.

5. George W. Bishop, Jr., *Charles H. Dow and the Dow Theory* (New York: Appleton-Century-Crofts, 1960), p. 121.

6. Richard Russell, "The Four Greatest Calls in Stock Market History," Dow Theory Letters, ww2.dowtheoryletters.com.

7. Ravi Nagarajan, "Net Current Asset Value Stocks," www.rationalwalk .com, March 14, 2009.

8. Seth Klarman, "The Forgotten Lessons of 2008," from his 2009 letter to shareholders, reprinted in *Value Investor Insight*, February 28, 2010, p. 22.

Chapter 3: Virtues and Vices of Graham's Philosophy

1. Benjamin Graham, *The Intelligent Investor* (New York: Harper & Row, 1973), p. 287.
2. Benjamin Graham, "Renaissance of Value," *Barron's*, September 23, 1974.
3. Benjamin Graham, speech at the National Federation of Financial Analysts Societies convention, 1958.
4. Dorothee Enskog, "Rethinking Risk Governance Following the Crisis," emagazine.credit-suisse.com, January 12, 2008.
5. Janet Lowe, *Value Investing Made Easy* (New York: McGraw-Hill, 1996), p. ix.
6. Charles T. Munger, comments at the Berkshire Hathaway annual meeting, Omaha, Nebraska, May 2, 2009.
7. Warren Buffett, comments at the Berkshire Hathaway annual meeting, Omaha, Nebraska, May 2, 2009.
8. Irving Janis, *Groupthink*, 2nd ed. (Boston: Houghton Mifflin, 1983).
9. Brandes Investment Partners, "Does Buy and Hold Still Work?" *The Focus*, November 2009.
10. Whitney Tilson and John Heins, "Buy and Hold Is Risky," *Kiplinger's Personal Finance*, March 2010.
11. Ibid.
12. Brandes Investment Partners, "Value Investing During and After U.S. Recessions: A Historical Perspective," 2008.
13. Ibid.

Chapter 4: Mr. Market

1. Jim Ware, *Investment Leadership: Building a Winning Culture for Long-Term Success* (Hoboken, NJ: John Wiley & Sons, 2004), p. v.
2. George W. Bishop, Jr., *Charles H. Dow and the Dow Theory* (New York: Appleton-Century Crofts, 1960), p. 106.
3. Benjamin Graham, *The Intelligent Investor* (New York: Harper & Brothers, 1954), p. 109.
4. Ibid., p. 138.
5. "Do Day Traders Make Money?" Investor Home, www.investorhome .com.

6. Ronald L. Johnson, "Day Trading: An Analysis of Public Day Trading at a Retail Day Trading Firm," www.nasaa.org/content/files/day_trading/analysis.pdf.

7. "Do Day Traders Make Money?" Investor Home, www.investorhome .com.

8. Philip A. Feigin, "Day Trading Craze Should Give Investors Pause," NASAA, November 25, 1998.

9. Bryant Urstadt, "Trading Shares in Milliseconds," www .technologyreview.com.

10. Richard Russell, "The Four Greatest Calls in Stock Market History," Dow Theory Letters, ww2.dowtheoryletters.com.

11. James Grant, *Minding Mr. Market* (New York: Farrar, Straus and Giroux, 1993), p. xv.

12. Warren E. Buffett, "Buy American, I Am," *The New York Times*, October 17, 2008.

13. Ibid.

14. David Iben, "A Penny for Your Thoughts," Tradewinds Global Investors newsletter, October 2008.

15. Brandes Investment Partners, "Message from Our Partners," First Quarter 2009.

16. Warren Buffett, 2009 letter to shareholders, p. 7.

Chapter 5: Risk Versus Reward

1. Suze Orman, "Ask Suze Orman," *The Costco Connection*, July 2009, p. 17.

2. Felix Salmon, "Recipe for Disaster: The Formula That Killed Wall Street," *Wired*, February 23, 2009.

3. David Iben, "Welcome to Hotel California," Tradewinds Global Investors newsletter, March 2008.

4. Bruce Grantier, "Benjamin Graham and Risk," Brandes Institute, 2009.

5. Seth Klarman, *Margin of Safety: Risk-Averse Value Investing Strategies for the Thoughtful Investor* (New York: Penguin Books, 1989), p. 171.

6. Ibid.

7. Charles Brandes, *Value Investing Today* (New York: McGraw-Hill, 2003).

8. Benjamin Graham, *The Intelligent Investor,* postscript to the revised edition (New York: HarperCollins, 2003).

9. John C. Bogle, " The Culture That Gave Rise to the Current Financial Crisis," speech at the seventh annual John M. Templeton, Jr., Lecture on Economic Liberties and the Constitution, Philadelphia, Pennsylvania, May 13, 2009.

10. *Value Investor Insight*, February 28, 2010, p. 1.

11. John C. Bogle, "Value Strategies," *The Wall Street Journal*, February 9, 2007, p. A11.

12. Ibid.

13. Warren E. Buffett, letter to shareholders, Berkshire Hathaway 2008 annual report, p. 17.

14. Ibid.

15. "Margin Account Debt on NYSE Stocks over $350 Billion—Record Debt Brings New Warnings of Risk," www.stockbrokerfraud.com, July 12, 2007.

16. Janet Lowe, *Value Investing Made Easy* (New York: McGraw-Hill, 1996).

Chapter 6: The Balance Sheet

1. David Iben, "Can You Hear Me, Major Tom?" Tradewinds Global Investors newsletter, June 2008.

2. Benjamin Graham, "Three Simple Methods of Common Stock Evaluation," 1975 speech.

3. Andrew Bary, "The Last Disciple," *Barron's*, March 13, 1995, p. 28.

4. Ibid.

5. Warren Buffett, 2009 letter to shareholders, p. 3.

6. Andrew Bary, "For Buffett Fans, the Price Is Right," onlinebarrons .com, July 14, 2009.

7. Lawrence J. White, "A New Law for the Bond Rating Industry," *Regulations,* The Cato Institute, Spring 2007.

8. "The Great Credit Rating Scandal," *MoneyWeek*, February 6, 2008, www.moneyweek.com.

9. Ibid.

10. Ravi Nagarajan, "Net Current Asset Value Stocks," www.rationalwalk .com, March 14, 2009.

11. Benjamin Graham and David Dodd, *Security Analysis* (New York: McGraw-Hill, 1940), p. 608.

Chapter 7: The Only Growth Rate That Counts: Earnings

1. A bow to Peter Lynch and the disclosure that this plays on a statement made by him.
2. Andrew Weiss, "The Guru of Value Investing Takes a Long View," *Hermes*, Fall 1994, p. 17.
3. Peter Lynch, *One Up on Wall Street* (New York: Penguin Books, 1989), p. 218.
4. Benjamin Graham, *The Intelligent Investor* (New York: Harper & Row, 1973), p. 178.
5. Lynch, *One Up on Wall Street*, p. 169.
6. Arthur Q. Johnson, Mundoval Fund newsletter, September 1, 2009.
7. Warren Buffett, 2009 letter to shareholders, p. 4.

Chapter 8: The Measure of Management

1. Warren Buffett, 2009 letter to shareholders, p. 3.
2. Warren Buffett, 1995 Berkshire Hathaway annual meeting.
3. A nod to author Sean Carroll and *The Colbert Report*, March 9, 2010.
4. Benjamin Graham and David Dodd, *Security Analysis* (New York: McGraw-Hill, 1940), p. 609.
5. Letter to the Securities and Exchange Commission, November 22, 2003, www.sec.gov/rules/proposed.
6. Charles Brandes, *Value Investing Today* (Homewood, IL: Dow Jones–Irwin, 1989,) p. 40.
7. Warren Buffett, 1994 Berkshire Hathaway annual meeting.
8. "What We Do," www.sec.gov.
9. John C. Bogle, "Restoring Faith in Financial Markets," *The Wall Street Journal*, January 19, 2010, p. A25.
10. Gretchen Morgenson, "John Bogle Doesn't Let Money Managers Off the Hook," *Fair Game*, April 12, 2009.
11. Michelle Leder, marketplace.publicradio.org, April 8, 2008.
12. Jorge E. Guerra, "The Sarbanes-Oxley Act and the Evolution of Corporate Governance," *CPA Journal*, March 2004.
13. Morgenson, "John Bogle Doesn't Let Money Managers Off the Hook."
14. Bogle, "Restoring Faith in Financial Markets."
15. Ibid.

16. Ibid.

17. "Wall Street Bonuses Shoot up 17 Percent in 2009," *Bozeman Daily Chronicle*, February 24, 2010.

18. Ravi Nagarajan, "Net Current Asset Value Stocks," www.rationalwalk.com, March 14, 2009.

Chapter 9: Stock Picking

1. Mario Gabelli blog, www.mariogabelliblog.com.

2. Benjamin Graham, "Current Problems in Security Analysis" (transcripts of lectures, September 1946–February 1947), p. 146.

3. Warren Buffett, comments at the Berkshire Hathaway annual meeting, Omaha, Nebraska, May 2, 2009.

4. David Iben, "When the Levee Breaks," Tradewinds Global Investors newsletter, December 2008.

5. Janet Lowe, *Benjamin Graham on Value Investing* (Chicago: Dearborn Financial Publishing, 1994), p. 218.

Chapter 10: Portfolio Requirements

1. From the private writings of Walter J. Schloss, CFA.

2. Seth Klarman, "The Forgotten Lessons of 2008," 2009 letter to shareholders, reprinted in *Value Investor Insight*, February 28, 2010, p. 22.

3. Warren Buffett, message to Buffett Limited Partnership, 1965.

4. Moshe A. Milevsky and Steven E. Posner, "A Continuous-Time Re-examination of the Inefficiency of Dollar-Cost Averaging," York University, Schulich School of Business, January 1999.

5. Benjamin Graham, "The Simplest Way to Select Bargain Stocks," special report, *Medical Economics*, September 20, 1976.

6. Warren Buffett, comments at the 1995 Berkshire Hathaway annual meeting.

7. Charles H. Brandes, *Value Investing Today* (Homewood, IL: Dow Jones–Irwin, 1989), p. 132.

8. Warren Buffett, 2009 letter to shareholders, p. 10.

9. David Iben, "When the Levee Breaks," Tradewinds Global Investors newsletter, December 2008.

10. Jim O'Neill, "Dreaming with the BRICS," global economics paper no. 99, Goldman Sachs, www2.goldmansachs.com.

11. Bill Barker, "The Performance of Mutual Funds," www.fool.com.

12. Benjamin Graham and David Dodd, *Security Analysis* (New York: McGraw-Hill, 1940), p. 594.

13. Selena Maranjian, "How I'm Grabbing 20% Dividend Yields," www .fool.com, May 11, 2009.

14. Brandes Investment Partners, "Does Buy and Hold Still Work?" *The Focus*, November 2009.

15. Ibid.

Chapter 11: Special Circumstances

1. Letter from the founders, "An Owner's Manual for Google's Shareholders," from the S-1 registration statement with the Securities and Exchange Commission. Available from several sources including www.Google.com.

2. Janet Lowe, *Google Speaks: Secrets of the World's Greatest Billionaire Entrepreneurs* (New York: John Wiley & Sons, 2008).

3. Jim Nelson, "4 Buyout Candidates You Need to Own for 2010," www .istockanalyst.com, December 23, 2000.

4. Bill Ackman, "Food for Thought," *Value Investor Insight*, February 28, 2010, p. 19.

5. Bill Mann, "When Companies Go Bankrupt," www.fool.com, September 16, 2008.

6. Ibid.

Chapter 12: Looking to Do Better

1. Jeff Sommer, "Extolling the Value of the Long View," *The New York Times*, October 26, 2008.

2. Robert Frank, "How a Secretary Made and Gave Away $17 Million," Wealth Report, WSJ Blogs, March 8, 2010.

3. "An Icy Outlook," Personal Business section, *Bloomberg Businessweek*, March 9, 2010, p. 67.

4. Comments at 1995 Berkshire Hathaway annual meeting.

5. Ibid.

6. "The Tractor Factor," Personal Business section, *Bloomberg Businessweek*, March 2010, p. 67.

7. Warren Buffett, letter to shareholders, Berkshire Hathaway annual report, 2008.

8. David Iben, "A Penny for Your Thoughts," Tradewinds Global Investors newsletter, October 2008.

9. David Iben, "When the Levee Breaks," Tradewinds Global Investors newsletter, December 2008.

10. Brandes Investment Partners, "A Message from Our Partners," First Quarter 2009.

11. David Iben, "Welcome to Hotel California," Tradewinds Global Investors newsletter, March 2008.

12. Warren Buffett, Comments at the Berkshire Hathaway annual meeting, Omaha, Nebraska, May 2, 2009.

13. Neil Irwin, "A Lost Decade for U.S. Economy, Workers," *The Washington Post*, January 2, 2010.

14. Ibid.

15. "The Forgotten Lessons of 2008," quoting from Seth Klarman's annual letter to shareholders, *Value Investor Insight*, February 28, 2010, p. 22.

16. George Papandreou, interview on *Charlie Rose*, PBS Television, March 9, 2010.

17. Luca DiLeo and Susanne Craig, "Fed Examines Swap Deals by Goldman and Others," *The Wall Street Journal*, February 20, 2010, p. A10.

Recommended Reading

Peter L. Bernstein. *Against the Gods: The Remarkable Story of Risk*. John Wiley & Sons, 1996.

Peter L. Bernstein. *Capital Ideas: The Improbable Origins of Modern Wall Street*. Maxwell Macmillan, 1992.

William Bernstein. *The Four Pillars of Investing: Lessons for Building a Winning Portfolio*. McGraw-Hill, 2002.

John C. Bogle. *The Little Book of Common Sense Investing: The Only Way to Guarantee Your Fair Share of Stock Market Returns*. John Wiley & Sons, 2007.

Charles Brandes. *Value Investing Today*. McGraw-Hill, 2003.

Christopher H. Browne. *The Little Book of Value Investing*. John Wiley & Sons, 2007.

Philip Carret. *The Art of Speculation*. Reprinted by Cosimo Classics in 2007. You may be able to locate a copy through a major library system or through a rare book dealer.

Robert Cialdini. *Influence: The Psychology of Persuasion*. Allyn & Bacon, 2001.

Ken Fisher. *How to Smell a Rat: The Five Signs of Financial Fraud*. John Wiley & Sons, 2009.

Philip Fisher. *Paths to Wealth Through Common Stocks*. Orignally published in 1960. Reprinted by John Wiley & Sons, 2007.

Benjamin Graham. *The Intelligent Investor*, 4th rev. ed. Harper & Row, 1973.

Benjamin Graham and David L. Dodd. *Security Analysis: Principles and Techniques*. McGraw-Hill, 1940.

Joel Greenblatt. *The Little Book That Beats the Market*. John Wiley & Sons, 2005.

Joel Greenblatt. *You Can Be a Stock Market Genius*. Simon & Schuster, 1997.

Bruce C. Greenwald et al. *Value Investing from Graham to Buffett and Beyond*. John Wiley & Sons, 2004.

Henry Hazlitt. *Economics in One Lesson: The Shortest and Surest Way to Understand Basic Economics.* First published in 1946; 50th anniversary edition. Fox & Wilkes, 1996.

Shefrin Hersh. *Beyond Greed and Fear: Understanding Behavioral Finance and the Psychology of Investing.* Oxford University Press, 2000.

Irving Janis. *Groupthink,* 2nd ed. Houghton Mifflin, 1983.

Charles P. Kindleberger. *Manias, Panics, and Crashes: A History of Financial Crises,* 5th ed. John Wiley & Sons, 2005.

Seth A. Klarman. *Margin of Safety: Risk-Averse Value Investing Strategies for the Thoughtful Investor.* Penguin Books, 1989.

Michael Lewis. *The Big Short: Inside the Doomsday Machine.* W. W. Norton, 2010.

Janet Lowe. *Benjamin Graham on Value Investing: Lessons from the Dean of Wall Street.* Dearborn, 1994.

Janet Lowe. *Damn Right: Behind the Scenes with Berkshire Billionaire Charlie Munger.* John Wiley & Sons, 2000.

Janet Lowe. *Value Investing Made Easy.* McGraw-Hill, 1996.

Janet Lowe. *Warren Buffett Speaks: Wit and Wisdom from the World's Greatest Investor,* rev. ed. John Wiley & Sons, 2007.

Roger Lowenstein. *Origins of the Crash: The Great Bubble and Its Undoing.* Penguin Books, 2004.

Roger Lowenstein. *When Genius Failed: The Rise and Fall of Long-Term Capital Management.* Random House, 2000.

Sebastian Mallaby. *More Money Than God: Hedge Funds and the Making of the New Elite.* Penguin Press, 2010.

William J. O'Neil. *How to Make Money in Stocks: A Winning System in Good Times or Bad,* 4th ed. McGraw-Hill, 2009.

William J. O'Neil. *The Successful Investor: What 80 Million People Need to Know to Invest Profitably and Avoid Big Losses.* McGraw-Hill, 2003.

Adam Smith. *Supermoney.* Random House, 1972.

www.amex.com—The American Stock Exchange Web site.

www.BerkshireHathaway.com—Warren Buffett's annual reports and other company information.

www.Brandes.com—Information on Brandes Investment Partners, reports on global investing and research by the Brandes Institute.

www.ccpg.org—Web site of the Connecticut Council on Problem Gambling. The council has worked with the Securities and Exchange Commission to study and address gambling in the stock market and provides valuable information and help related to the subject.

www.djaverages.com—Current and past information on performance of all of the Dow Jones averages.

www.fool.com— Web site of the Motley Fool, one of the Internet's most popular financial resources. The Motley Fool provides news, analysis, advice, and information on all types of investments.

www.footnoted.org—A Web site that scours, exposes, and explains footnotes in corporate SEC filings. This is an entertaining site and a good place to learn more about corporate governance.

www.investopedia.com—Information source for investors, including long lists of definitions, explanations, and financially related articles.

www.iqtrends.com—The Web site for the respected newsletter *Investment Quality Trends*. IQTrends has studied and tracked the importance, influence, and value of dividends for thirty years and offers information and guidance for those interested in both investment income and growth.

www.johncbogle.com—Discover what this pioneering, independent investor is thinking right now.

www.kiplinger.com—A useful site for information, but even more so for easy calculators covering various aspects of investing.

www.quantumonline.com—Information regarding preferred shares.

www.quicken.com—Quicken is the leader in personal financial software. Its products combine everything from your checkbook to investment accounts. At tax time, you can load data into its tax-preparation software.

www.savingsbonds.gov—Inflation, maturity dates, earnings calculators, and other information on U.S. savings bonds, which can sometimes be a surprisingly effective investment for individuals.

www.sec.gov—General information on rules, regulations, and governance for publicly traded U.S. corporations.

www.sec.gov/edgar—Documents and information related to publicly traded U.S. companies.

www.sec.gov/investor/pubs/—Great source of information on companies and guidance for individual investors. There are several useful articles on spotting and avoiding fraud.

www2.standardandpoors.com—Detailed information on S&P's many products and services, as well as detailed information on the indices.

www.treasurydirect.com—Open an account with the U.S. Treasury to buy and sell Treasury bills, notes, and bonds or savings bonds online. Funds transfer from and to your specified bank account.

www.valueinvestorinsight.com—The Web site for the magazine *Value Investor Insight*. The site offers a free sample copy of the most recent issue of the magazine.